Heritage BUILDERS

Family Night Tool Chest

Book 2

Basic Christian Beliefs

Creating Lasting Impressions for the Next Generation

Jim Weidmann and Kurt Bruner
with Mike and Amy Nappa

ChariotVICTOR
PUBLISHING
A DIVISION OF COOK COMMUNICATIONS

This book is dedicated in love to my mother and father,
JoAnn and Larry Weidmann,
who taught and modeled for me
the importance of family.
I have been blessed by
your parenting and your example.
—J.W.

Victor Books is an imprint of ChariotVictor Publishing,
a division of Cook Communications, Colorado Springs, Colorado 80918
Cook Communications, Paris, Ontario
Kingsway Communications, Eastbourne, England.

HERITAGE BUILDERS/FAMILY NIGHT TOOL CHEST, BOOK 2
© 1997 by Kurt Bruner and Jim Weidmann

First edition 1997

Edited by Eric Stanford
Design by Bill Gray
Cover and Interior Illustrations by Guy Wolek

ISBN 0-7814-097-X

Printed and bound in the United States of America
01 00 99 98 97   5 4 3 2

Heritage Builders/Family Night Tool Chest, Book 2, is a Heritage Builders book, created in association with the authors at Nappaland Communications. To contact Heritage Builders Association, send e-mail to: Hbuilders@aol.com.

Contents

Family Nights about Basic Christian Beliefs

The Heritage Builders Series

This resource was created as an outreach of the Heritage Builders Association—a network of families and churches committed to passing a strong heritage to the next generation. Designed to motivate and assist families as they become intentional about the heritage passing process, this series draws upon the collective wisdom of parents, grandparents, church leaders, and family life experts, in an effort to provide balanced, biblical parenting advice along with effective, practical tools for family living. For more information on the goals and work of the Heritage Builders Association, please see page 122.

Kurt Bruner, M.A.
Executive Editor
Heritage Builders Series

✆ Introduction

There is toothpaste all over the plastic covered table. Four young kids are having the time of their lives squeezing the paste out of the tube—trying to expunge every drop like Dad told them to. "Okay," says Dad, slapping a twenty-dollar bill onto the table. "The first person to get the toothpaste back into their tube gets this money!" Little hands begin working to shove the peppermint pile back into rolled up tubes—with very limited success.

Jim is in the midst of a weekly routine in the Weidmann home when he and his wife spend time creating "impression points" with the kids. "We can't do it, Dad!" protests the youngest child.

"The Bible tells us that's just like your tongue. Once the words come out, it's impossible to get them back in. You need to be careful what you say because you may wish you could take it back." An unforgettable impression is made.

Impression points occur every day of our lives. Intentionally or not, we impress upon our children our values, preferences, beliefs, quirks and concerns. It happens both through our talk and through our walk. When we do it right, we can turn them on to the things we believe. But when we do it wrong, we can turn them off to the values we most hope they will embrace. The goal is to find ways of making this reality work for us, rather than against us. How? By creating and capturing opportunities to impress upon the next generation our values and beliefs. In other words, through what we've labeled impression points.

The kids are all standing at the foot of the stairs. Jim is at the top of that same staircase. They wait eagerly for Dad's instructions.

"I'll take you to Baskin Robbins for ice cream if you can figure how to get up here." He has the attention of all four kids. "But there are a few rules. First, you can't touch the stairs. Second, you can't touch the railing. Now, begin!"

After several contemplative moments, the youngest speaks up. "That's impossible Dad! How can we get to where you are without touching the stairs or the railing?"

After some disgruntled agreement from two of the other children, Jacob gets an idea. "Hey, Dad. Come down here." Jim walks down the stairs. "Now bend over while I get on your back. Okay, climb the stairs."

Bingo! Jim proceeds to parallel this simple game with how it is impossible to get to God on our own. But when we trust Christ's completed work on our behalf, we can get to heaven. A lasting impression is made. After a trip up the stairs on Dad's back, the whole gang piles into the minivan for a double scoop of mint-chip.

Six years ago, Jim and his wife Janet began setting aside time to intentionally impress upon the kids their values and beliefs through a weekly ritual called "family night." They play games, talk, study, and do the things which reinforce the importance of family and faith. It is during these times that they intentionally create these impression points with their kids. The impact? The kids are having fun and a heritage is being passed.

☙ intentional or "oops"?

Sometimes, we accidentally impress the wrong things on our kids rather than intentionally impressing the right things. But there is an effective, easy way to change that. Routine family nights are a powerful tool for creating intentional impression points with our children.

The concept behind family nights is rooted in a biblical mandate summarized in Deuteronomy 6:5-9.

> *"Love the Lord your God with all your heart and with all your soul and with all your strength. These commandments that I give you today are to be upon your hearts. Impress them on your children!"*
> ***How?***
> *"Talk about them when you sit at home and when you walk along the road, when you lie down and when you get up. Tie them as symbols on your hands and bind them on your foreheads. Write them on the doorframes of your houses and on your gates."*

In other words, we need to take advantage of every opportunity to impress our beliefs and values in the lives of our children. A growing network of parents are discovering family nights to be a highly effective, user-friendly approach to doing just that. As one father put it . . . " This has changed our entire family life." And another dad . . . " Our investment of time and energy into family nights has more eternal value than we may ever know." Why? Because they are intentionally teaching their children at the wisdom level, the level at which the children understand and can apply.

☺ truth is a treasure

Two boys are running all over the house, carefully following the complex and challenging instructions spelled out on the "truth treasure map" they received moments ago. An earlier map contained a few rather simple instructions that were much easier to follow. But the "false treasure box" it lead to left something to be desired. It was empty. Boo Dad! They hope for a better result with map number two.

STEP ONE:

Walk sixteen paces into the front family room.

STEP TWO:

Spin around seven times, then walk down the stairs.

STEP THREE:

Run backwards to the other side of the room.

STEP FOUR:

Try and get around Dad and climb under the table.

You get the picture. The boys are laughing at themselves, complaining to Dad, and having a ball. After twenty minutes treasure hunting they finally reach the elusive "truth treasure box." Little hands open the lid, hoping for a better result this time around. They aren't disappointed. The box contains a nice selection of their favorite candies. Yeah Dad!

"Which map was easier to follow?" Dad asks.

"The first one." comes their response.

"Which one was better?"

"The second one. It led to a true treasure," says the oldest.

"That's just like life," Dad shares, "Sometimes it's easier to follow what is false. But it is always better to seek and follow what is true."

They read from Proverbs 2 about the hidden treasure of God's truth and we end their time repeating tonight's jingle—"It's best for you to seek what's true." Then they indulge themselves with a mouthful of delicious candy!

℮ the power of family nights

The power of family nights is twofold. First, it creates a formal setting within which Dad and Mom can intentionally instill beliefs, values or character qualities within their child. Rather than defer to the influence of peers and media, or abdicate character training to the school and church, parents create the opportunity to teach their children the things that matter most.

The second impact of family nights is perhaps even more significant than the first. Twenty to sixty minutes of formal fun and instruction can set up countless opportunities for informal reinforcement. These informal impression points do not have to be created, they just happen—at the dinner table, while driving in the car, while watching television, or any other parent/child time together. Once you have formally discussed a given family night topic, you and your children will naturally refer back to those principles during the routine dialogues of everyday life.

If the truth were known, many of us hated family devotions while growing up. We had them sporadically at best, usually whenever our parents were feeling particularly guilty. But that was fine, since the only thing worse was a trip to the dentist. Honestly, do we really think that is what God had in mind when He instructed us to teach our children? As an alternative, many parents are discovering family nights to be a wonderful complement to or replacement for family devotions as a means of passing their beliefs and values to the kids. In fact, many parents hear their kids ask at least three times per week

"Can we have family night tonight?"

Music to Dad's and Mom's ears!

⊙ Keys to Effective Family Nights

There are several keys which should be incorporated into effective family nights.

MAKE IT FUN!

Enjoy yourself, and let the kids have a ball. They may not remember everything you say, but they will always cherish the times of laughter—and so will you.

KEEP IT SIMPLE!

The minute you become sophisticated or complicated, you've missed the whole point. Don't try to create deeply profound lessons. Just try to reinforce your values and beliefs in a simple, easy to understand manner. Read short passages, not long, drawn out sections of Scripture. Remember: The goal is to keep it simple.

DON'T DOMINATE!

You want to pull them into the discovery process as much as possible. If you do all the talking, you've missed the mark. Ask questions, give assignments, invite participation in every way possible. They will learn more when you involve all of their senses and emotions.

GO WITH THE FLOW!

It's fine to start with a well defined outline, but don't kill spontaneity by becoming overly structured. If an incident or question brings you a different direction, great! Some of the best impression opportunities are completely unplanned and unexpected.

MIX IT UP!

Don't allow yourself to get into a rut or routine. Keep the sense of excitement and anticipation through variety. Experiment to discover what works best for your family. Use books, games, videos, props, made up stories, songs, music or music videos, or even go on a family outing.

DO IT OFTEN!

We tend to find time for the things that are really important. It is best to set aside one evening per week (the same evening if possible) for family night. Remember, repetition is the best teacher. The more impressions you can create, the more of an impact you will make.

MAKE A MEMORY!

Find ways to make the lesson stick. For example, just as advertisers create"jingles" to help us remember their products, it is helpful to create family night "jingles" to remember the main theme—such as "It's best for you, to seek what's true" or "Just like air, God is there!"

USE OTHER TOOLS FROM THE HERITAGE BUILDERS TOOL CHEST!

Family night is only one exciting way for you to intentionally build a loving heritage for your family. You'll also want to use these other exciting tools from Heritage Builders.

The Family Fragrance: There are five key qualities to a healthy family fragrance, each contributing to an environment of love in the home. It's easy to remember the Fragrance Five by fitting them into an acrostic using the word "Aroma"—

A—Affection
R—Respect
O—Order
M—Merriment
A—Affirmation

Traditions: Meaningful activities which the process of passing on emotional, spiritual, and relational inheritance between generations. Family traditions can play a vital role in this process.

The Right Angle: The Right Angle is the standard of normal healthy living against which our children will be able to measure their atttitudes, actions, and beliefs.

Impression Points: Ways that we impress on our children our values, preferences, and concerns. We do it through our talk and our actions. We do it intentionally (through such methods as Family Nights), and we do it incidentally.

Please see the back of the book for information on how to receive the FREE Heritage Builders Newsletter which contains more information about these exciting tools! Also, look for the new book, *The Heritage*, available at your local Christian bookstore.

How to Use This Tool Chest

Summary page: For those who like the bottom line, we have provided a summary sheet at the start of each family night session. This abbreviated version of the topic briefly highlights the goal, key Scriptures, activity overview, main points, and life slogan. On the reverse side of this detachable page there is space provided for you to write down any ideas you wish to add or alter as you make the lesson your own.

Step-by-step: For those seeking suggestions and directions for each step in the family night process, we have provided a section which walks you through every activity, question, Scripture reading, and discussion point. Feel free to follow each step as written as you conduct the session, or read through this portion in preparation for your time together.

A la carte: We strongly encourage you to use the material in this book in an "a la carte" manner. In other words, pick and choose the questions, activities, Scriptures, age appropriate ideas, etc. which best fit your family. This book is not intended to serve as a curriculum, requiring compliance with our sequence and plan, but rather as a tool chest from which you can grab what works for you and which can be altered to fit your family situation.

The long and the short of it: Each family night topic presented in this book includes several activities, related Scriptures, and possible discussion items. Do not feel it is necessary to conduct them all in a single family night. You may wish to spread one topic over several weeks using smaller portions of each chapter, depending upon the attention span of the kids and the energy level of the parents. Remember, short and effective is better than long and thorough.

Journaling: Finally, we have provided space with each session for you to capture a record of meaningful comments, funny happenings, and unplanned moments which will inevitably occur during family night. Keep a notebook of these journal entries for future reference. You will treasure this permanent record of the heritage passing process for years to come.

☉ 1: Great Big Know-It-All

Exploring God's omniscience

Scripture
• Psalm 139:2-4—God knows everything about us.
• Matthew 10:30—God knows even the number of hairs on our heads!
• Isaiah 40:13-14—God has never needed a teacher.
• Ephesians 1:4-6—God knew us before Creation.
• Jeremiah 29:11—God knows the future.

ACTIVITY OVERVIEW		
Activity	Summary	Pre-Session Prep
Activity 1: When I Was Your Age . . .	Remember the past and dream of the future.	You'll need no supplies.
Activity 2: Mind Reader	Participate in a mind-reading trick.	You'll need 3-by-5-inch cards, a pen, and a Bible.
Activity 3: The Big Picture	Compare a puzzle to God's view of our lives.	You'll need two puzzles and a Bible.

Main Points:
—God knows everything!
—God knows all about you and me.
—God knows His plans for our us in the future.

LIFE SLOGAN: "Future, present, or past, God's knowledge will always last!"

Make it your own
In the space provided below, outline the flow and add any additional ideas to guide you through the process of conducting this family night.

Prayer & Praise Items
In the space provided below, list any items you wish to pray about or give praise for during this family night session.

Journal
In the space provided below, capture a record of what fun or meaningful things which happened during this family night session.

Session Tip

We intentionally have provided more material than we would expect to be used in a single "Family Night" session. You know your family's unique interests and life circumstances best, so feel free to adapt this session to meet your family members' needs. Remember, short and simple is better than long and comprehensive.

WARM-UP

Open with Prayer: Begin by having a family member pray, asking God to help everyone in the family understand more about Him through this time. After prayer, review your last lesson by asking these questions:

- **What did we learn about in our last lesson?**
- **What was the Life Slogan?**
- **Have your actions changed because of what we learned? If so, how?** Encourage family members to give specific examples of how they've applied learning from the past week.

Share: Today we're going to discover what it means to know everything!

ACTIVITY 1: When I Was Your Age...

Point: God knows everything!

Activity: Begin your time by telling your children about your own childhood. Briefly explain some of the differences between life then and life now. This doesn't have to be a sob story about how you had to walk three miles to school, barefoot in the snow, uphill both ways! Instead, share about how things were different.

Depending on your age, you might not have had items that are common today, such as a microwave oven, dishwasher, color television, computer, videos, compact discs, cable television, pocket calculators, and so on. Your children may have a hard time understanding what life was like without these things.

You can also share about how society has changed. More mothers stayed at home years ago; there was less crime, less pollution, more racism, less divorce, fewer cures for sickness, and so on. Some changes have been for the better, while some haven't.

After sharing about yourself, discuss these questions:
- **Who's the oldest person you know? What do you think life was like for this person?**
- **Now let's move from the past into the future. What kind of changes do you think will happen in the next 20 years? What will life be like for your children?**

If your kids give vague, "I don't know" answers, ask more specific questions, such as "What do you think a bathroom will be like in 20 years? What do you think a playground will be like in 20 years? a kitchen? fast food? newspapers? Will there still be poor people? sick people?" and so on.

After your discussion, share: None of us knows exactly what the future will be like. And no one living can tell us exactly about the distant past. Scientists and researchers make their best guesses about dinosaurs and life hundreds and thousands of years ago, but they don't know exactly what the past was like. They weren't there. But God was! God was in the past, exists right now, and already knows the future.

Take some time to imagine all the things God's known about in the past. He knew every dinosaur, every soldier in past wars. God knows the true date the earth was created. He even knows who really shot JFK! He knew your great-great-greatgrandparents, He knows you, and He already knows your great-great-great-grandchildren!

Share: God knows everything! This is called omniscience. *Omni* means "everything" or "all," and *science* means "knowledge." What does this mean to you?

Possible answers are:
- Nobody has to teach God.
- God has known all there is to know, always.
- Humans are still learning about the body, earth, space, oceans, and so on. God already knows it all!

Age Adjustments

SCHOOL-AGED CHILDREN may enjoy further learning about what life was like in the past. Books such as the "Little House" series give a taste of how life was different years ago. Or children might like to interview elderly family members or neighbors to find out how their lives have changed. The idea of grandmom riding a horse to school might be exciting, but the thought of her washing her clothes in a pot over the stove might not be as thrilling!

Children may also be interested in reading books in which people have tried to predict the future. Jules Verne books or science fiction related to the future may capture their interests. Challenge children to question which predictions have come true, such as flying machines or submarines, and which have yet to happen. Through it all, bring out the point that God already knows what *really* happens.

- God started all knowledge. He put all the laws in place at the beginning of time.
- God's knowledge is completely different from ours. He's not bound by time, space, or earthly laws like we are.

ACTIVITY 2: Mind Reader

Point: God knows all about you and me.

 Supplies: You'll need 3-by-5-inch cards, a pen, and a Bible.

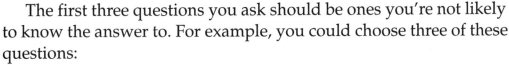

Activity: Explain that you'd like to demonstrate how much you know about your children with a "magic" trick. Ask one child to be your volunteer for this trick.

Explain: **I'm going to ask you four questions, and before you answer, I'll write down how I think you're going to answer. Then you can tell me what your answer was. After we've gone through all four questions, we'll see how well I could predict your answers.**

The first three questions you ask should be ones you're not likely to know the answer to. For example, you could choose three of these questions:

- What did you eat for lunch today?
- Who sits next to you in school?
- What color is your chair at school?
- Where do you hope we'll go on vacation this summer?
- If you could buy any toy, what would you buy?

The fourth question should be one *you're sure you know the answer to.* For example:

- If you could go to Disneyland tomorrow or go to school, which would you choose?
- If you could have asparagus or a hot fudge sundae for dessert, which would you choose?

Again, this should be a question for which you're sure you'll correctly guess your child's answer.

Now, here's how the trick works.

1. Ask the first question, such as "If you could buy any toy, what would you buy?"

2. Before your child answers, write down *what you think he or*

she will answer for the fourth *question,* such as "I'd rather go to Disneyland," and place this facedown on the table. Don't say anything aloud.

Age Adjustments

FOR YOUNGER CHILDREN, play a game with three small boxes, such as shoe boxes, and a small toy. Place the boxes in a line with the open sides facing in the same direction. Without the children looking, put the toy in one box. Then allow one child to stand in front of the open boxes while the other children face closed cardboard. Those facing the closed sides will have to guess where the toy is, but the one facing the open sides will already know. You can play this game again and again, letting a different child stand at the open sides each time.

After the game, compare this to how God can see everything and knows everything, even though we don't know everything.

FOR OLDER CHILDREN AND TEENAGERS, find a book explaining Bible prophecies of the Old Testament that came true in the New Testament. How does this prove that God knows the future?

3. Now that you've written an answer, let your child answer the *first* question aloud. Let's say his or her answer is "I'd buy a new video-game system."

4. Ask the second question, such as "What did you eat for lunch today?"

5. Before your child answers, write down his or her *answer to the* first *question*, "I'd buy a new video-game system," and place that in the stack with the first card.

6. Now let your child answer the second question aloud.

Continue in this manner, always writing down the answer to the *previous* question, until you have four cards in the stack. Then turn them over and read what you've written in the order you asked the questions. You can then hand the cards to your child as proof that you answered the questions correctly.

If the kids are mystified, try the trick again on another child. If your child for some reason answers the last question in a way you didn't predict (like he or she actually chose school over Disneyland), you'll still have three correct answers, which is a pretty good ratio!

After you've had fun with this, see if the kids can guess how you did this. Finally, explain the trick so they can try it on their friends at a later date. Then question them:

- **Did you think I could really read your mind?**
- **Is there anyone who could know *everything* about you? what you dream about? what you hope for? your secrets?**

Share: God knows everything about us! He knows our likes, dislikes, good and bad habits, what we believe in, everything! Let's look for some examples of this in the Bible.

 Read the following verses, and after each one ask: **What does this verse tell us about what God knows?**

- Psalm 139:2-4 (God knows when we sit, when we stand, what our thoughts are, when we are at home, where we go; God knows what we're going to say even before we say it.)
- Matthew 10:30 (God knows even the number of hairs on our heads.)
- Isaiah 40:13-14 (No one has taught God; God didn't consult anyone and still doesn't; God knows everything without us telling Him anything.)
- Ephesians 1:4-6 (God knew us and chose us before the world was even created.)

ACTIVITY 3: The Big Picture

Point: God knows His plans for us in the future.

 Supplies: You'll need two puzzles and a Bible.

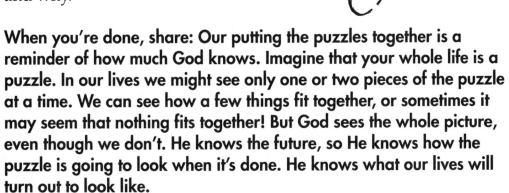

Activity: Bring out two relatively simple puzzles. Form two teams (a team can be one person if your family is small). Have one team put their puzzle together with the picture facing up, and the other put theirs together with the picture facing down. See which way takes longer. If you like, teams can switch puzzles so they see what it's like doing the puzzle both ways. Discuss which way of putting the puzzle together is harder, and why.

When you're done, share: Our putting the puzzles together is a reminder of how much God knows. Imagine that your whole life is a puzzle. In our lives we might see only one or two pieces of the puzzle at a time. We can see how a few things fit together, or sometimes it may seem that nothing fits together! But God sees the whole picture, even though we don't. He knows the future, so He knows how the puzzle is going to look when it's done. He knows what our lives will turn out to look like.

Read Jeremiah 29:11 and ask:
- **How does this verse make you feel about God?**
- **How does it make you feel about tomorrow? next year? 20 years from now?**

Share: God knows everything, and God knows His plans for us. We have to trust that since God can see the whole picture of our lives, He knows where we're going and what we should be doing.

WRAP-UP

Gather everyone in a circle and have family members take turns answering this question: **What's one thing you've learned about God today?**

Next, tell kids you've got a new "Life Slogan" you'd like to share with them.

Life Slogan: Today's Life Slogan is this: "Future, present, or past, God's knowledge will always last!" Have family members repeat the slogan two or three times to help them learn it. Then encourage them to practice saying it during the week so they can talk about it at your next family night session.

Close in Prayer: Allow time for each family member to share prayer concerns and answers to prayer. Then close your time together with prayer for each concern. Thank God for listening to and caring about us.

Remember to record your prayer requests so you can refer to them in the future as you see God answering them.

Additional Resources:

Have You Seen the Wind? by Kathleen Crawford (ages 4–8)

2: Spittin' Image

Exploring what it means to be created in God's image and what happened when sin entered the human race

Scripture
- Genesis 1:24-27—God made us in His image.
- Genesis 3:1-24—Sin separates humanity from God.

ACTIVITY OVERVIEW		
Activity	Summary	Pre-Session Prep
Activity 1: Spittin' Image	Learn what it takes to be in someone's image.	You'll need a large paper roll and some crayons or markers. Also, pictures of your kids and of yourself as a child.
Activity 2: Formed by God	Learn what it means to be made in God's image.	You'll need play dough and a Bible.
Activity 3: Blocked from View	Understand how sin blocks us from God.	You'll need a Bible and the creations from your last activity.

Main Points:
- —God created us in His own image
- —Sin separates us from God.

LIFE SLOGAN: "God made you and God made me so His children we could be."

Make it your own
In the space provided below, outline the flow and add any additional ideas to guide you through the process of conducting this family night.

Prayer & Praise Items
In the space provided below, list any items you wish to pray about or give praise for during this family night session.

Journal
In the space provided below, capture a record of what fun or meaningful things which happened during this family night session.

Session Tip

We intentionally have provided more material than we would expect to be used in a single "Family Night" session. You know your family's unique interests and life circumstances best, so feel free to adapt this session to meet your family members' needs. Remember, short and simple is better than long and comprehensive.

 WARM-UP

Open with Prayer: Begin by having a family member pray, asking God to help everyone in the family understand more about Him through this time. After prayer, review your last lesson by asking these questions:

- **What did we learn about in our last lesson?**
- **What was the Life Slogan?**
- **Have your actions changed because of what we learned? If so, how?** Encourage family members to give specific examples of how they've applied learning from the past week.

ACTIVITY 1: Spittin' Image

Point: If you are in someone else's image, that means you look like that person.

Supplies: You'll need a paper roll or several connected papers large enough to trace each child's body. You'll also need crayons or markers, and pictures of the kids and pictures of yourself as a child.

Activity: Unroll the large paper on the floor. Ask each child to lie down on the paper so that you can trace their image. After tracing the image of their body onto the paper, give each child crayons or markers and ask them to fill in the image by adding a face, clothes, etc.

Direct them to make the image on the page look as much like themselves as possible perhaps by copying the clothes they are wearing, hair color and length, shoes, etc.

Ask this question:
- **Who's image is the drawing on the paper?**

Explain that to be in the image of someone means to look like them. Share that each child is, in at least a small way, in the image of Mom and/or Dad. (If you have pictures from when you were a child, show them alongside each child's picture and point out any similarities. If there aren't many, be creative!) Make the point that to be in the image of someone means to be like them.

Discuss this question:
- **Why do you think children sometimes look like their parents?** (Because they are in the image of their parents.)

ACTIVITY 2: Formed by God

Point: God created us in His own image.

 Supplies: You'll need play dough or clay and a Bible.

Activity: Give each family member a handful of play dough or clay.

Share: Use your play dough to make a picture or sculpture that looks as much like you as possible.

Give everyone plenty of time to model their images. If you like, you might also provide rolling pins, cookie cutters, knives, or other objects that might help in the creative process.

When all the self-portraits are complete, take a few minutes to admire and compliment each other's work. Then discuss:
- **How are these sculptures like and unlike the real you?**

Share: This activity makes me think of how God formed us.

 Read Genesis 1:24-27 aloud, then ask the following questions:
- **What does it mean to be created in someone's image?** (To be made like them, to look like them.)
- **We tried to make sculptures of our own images. How is this like when God created**

Age Adjustments

CHILDREN OF ALL AGES will enjoy the process of tracing, coloring, and creating images of themselves. FOR OLDER CHILDREN, however, you may want to have them attempt to create shadow images of one another for an added challenge.

us in His image? (He formed us to be like Himself.)
• **How are we like God?**

In your discussion, bring out these three ways we are like God:
1. People were created with a mind. Our brain gives us the abilities to think and learn. Our minds are different from those of animals, which God gave us the responsibility of ruling. We were created higher than the animals and have the ability to understand and communicate with God.
2. People were created with a soul. This is also sometimes referred to as a "heart." We have our physical hearts, the muscle that pumps blood through our bodies, but we also have a soul. This is what makes you unique, what makes you you!
3. People were created with a will. This means we can choose to do things God's way or our own way. When we do things that are not God's way, we are sinning.

Share: When we created our sculptures, we were limited in how good a job we could do. But God wasn't limited when He made us. He made us like Himself in many ways!

 Question:
Do we look like God?

Answer: God is a Spirit, so He doesn't have a physical body. However, we know that we have physical parts that reflect Him in several ways. Just as God can hear, for example, so He gave us physical ears so that we too can hear. God sees, so He gave us eyes. In these and other ways, we "look" like God!

ACTIVITY 3: Blocked from View

Point: Sin separates us from God.

 Supplies: You'll need a Bible, the creations made in the previous activity, and a piece of dried, hardened play dough or clay.

Share: The first people God made in His image, Adam and Eve, were the closest any people have ever been to being like God, because they had never sinned. We can read in the Bible of how the first sin happened and what the results were.

Read Genesis 3:1-24 aloud, then discuss the following questions:

- **How can you summarize what happened here in your own words?**
- **How were Adam and Eve different after they had sinned?** (They knew they were naked; they were ashamed; they were afraid of God.)
- **In what ways would they, and all people born after them, never be the same?** (They would always have to deal with the result of sin—separation from God.)

Share: Simply put, God and humans had a perfect relationship before they sinned. Adam and Eve would talk to God, and perhaps even see God. But after Adam and Eve sinned, there was a "wall" between God and humans. God is perfect and can't have sin in His presence. So Adam and Eve, and all humans after them, couldn't have the same kind of relationship with God that they had before. Sin separates us from God.

To demonstrate this reality, have family members hide their creations where they cannot be seen. This might be under a chair, under a bowl, or covered with a cloth.

Next, show the children the hardened piece of clay.

Share: When clay is exposed to air for a long time, it gets hard. In the same way, our hearts (or souls) can become hard when we're exposed to sin. The more we live in sin, the more exposed we are to that which will make our hearts hard toward God.

- **In what ways do you think sin makes us "hard" toward God?** (We don't want to be close to Him because we are ashamed. We don't listen to Him because we want to do what we know is wrong.)

Share: We were created by God in His image to be His children and to have a loving relationship with Him. But sin created a wall between God and us, so that relationship was broken. But God still loves us and wants us to be His children again! We will learn more about how in a future family night.

WRAP-UP

Gather everyone in a circle and have family members take turns answering this question: **What's one thing you've learned about God today?**

Next, tell kids you've got a new "Life Slogan" you'd like to share with them.

Life Slogan: Today's Life Slogan is this: "God made you and God made me so His children we could be." Have family members repeat the slogan two or three times to help them learn it. Then encourage them to practice saying it during the week so they can talk about it at your next family night session.

**Close in Prayer:** Allow time for each family member to share prayer concerns and answers to prayer. Then close your time together with prayer for each concern. Thank God for listening to and caring about us.

Remember to record your prayer requests so you can refer to them in the future as you see God answering them.

Additional Resources:

Who Made the Morning? by Jan Godfrey (ages 4–8)
Little Mouse Library by Barbara Davoll (ages 1–3)

⊚ 3: Do I Know You?

Exploring the difference between knowing about God and knowing God

Scripture:
- 1 John 4:7-12—We know God better by loving others.
- James 4:8—God wants us to get closer to Him.
- John 10:1-6—The more we know God, the more we know His voice.

ACTIVITY OVERVIEW

Activity	Summary	Pre-Session Prep
Activity 1: In the Know	Discover the difference between knowing someone and knowing about them.	You'll need copies of the questionnaire on page 38, pencils, and a Bible.
Activity 2: God's Treasure	Learn that the Bible is a treasure chest full of information about how to know God.	You'll need a hidden Bible and clues leading to the Bible.
Activity 3: Who Said That?	Explore how we recognize the voices of those we spend time with.	You'll need a Bible.

Main Points:

—We know others by our relationships with them.
—Reading God's Word is one way to get to know God.
—The more we know God, the more we know God's voice.

LIFE SLOGAN: "To love Him is to know Him!"

Make it your own

In the space provided below, outline the flow and add any additional ideas to guide you through the process of conducting this family night.

Prayer & Praise Items

In the space provided below, list any items you wish to pray about or give praise for during this family night session.

Journal

In the space provided below, capture a record of what fun or meaningful things which happened during this family night session.

Session Tip

We intentionally have provided more material than we would expect to be used in a single "Family Night" session. You know your family's unique interests and life circumstances best, so feel free to adapt this session to meet your family members' needs. Remember, short and simple is better than long and comprehensive.

WARM-UP

Open with Prayer: Begin by having a family member pray, asking God to help everyone in the family understand more about Him through this time. After prayer, review your last lesson by asking these questions:

- **What do you remember from our last lesson?**
- **What thought from our last lesson has stuck with you this week?**
- **Have your actions changed over the last week because of anything we learned? If so, how?**
- **Do you remember the Life Slogan?**

Share: This week we're going to learn about how we can know God. Let's get started!

ACTIVITY 1: In the Know

Point: We know others by our relationships with them.

Supplies: You'll need copies of the questionnaire on page 38, pencils, and a Bible. You'll also need to make arrangements ahead of time with a friend, whom we'll call "Bob" during this lesson. (You can fill in the name of the actual friend whenever you see "Bob.") Choose a friend whom your children have heard you talk about but whom your children don't know themselves. This might be an associate from work whom your children have met when visiting you at the office but with whom they've never had an extended conversation. Arrange for this person to be available for your phone call during family night.

Activity: Give each family member a copy of the questionnaire on page 38 and a pencil. Explain that each person is to fill out the questionnaire about himself or herself. Don't allow any talking or sharing of answers. If you have children too young to write, you can quietly help them fill in their questionnaires.

When everyone is done, begin with yourself. **Ask: What makes me mad?**

Give each person a chance to tell what they think makes you mad, then share what you wrote about yourself on your questionnaire. See how well the answers they shared and what you wrote match. You might also find you agree with what was said about you, even though you forgot to write that down. Remember to keep a spirit of fun about this activity, rather than one of criticism.

Move on to the next question, again letting everyone else share their thoughts about you before you reveal what you actually wrote. When all the questions on your paper have been covered, go to the next family member. Continue in the same manner with this person, then move on until each family member has been discussed.

Explain: **Now we're going to fill out a questionnaire on "Bob."**

Without offering any of your knowledge of Bob, have family members fill out a questionnaire telling how they think Bob will answer these questions. Don't get bogged down if kids complain about not knowing the answers. Just encourage them to make their best guesses from what they've heard you say about Bob in the past.

When the questions have been answered, call Bob and have him share his answers to the questions. If you have a speaker phone, or can borrow one for this activity, it would be fun to let everyone hear the answers straight from Bob's mouth. If a speaker phone isn't available, have the person talking to Bob relay his answers back to the rest of the family.

If you like, tell Bob what your family members thought or guessed about him.

After the conversation, thank Bob and hang up. Then discuss these questions:

- **How good were our guesses about Bob?**
- **What could have made our answers closer to his answers?**
- **Why were we able to answer more closely on questions**

about family members, while we had so much trouble with Bob?

Share: The difference between these two situations is that we are close to each other. We spend time together. We have relationships with each other. We *know* each other. None of you spend time with Bob. None of you has a relationship with him. You may have heard me talk about Bob, so you know a little bit *about* him, but you don't *know* him.

Ask this question: **How is this like the difference between knowing God and knowing about God?** (Just as we can only know other people by having a relationship with them, so the only way we can really know God is to have a relationship with Him.)

Age Adjustments

FOR YOUNGER CHILDREN, shorten the questionnaire, focusing on only two or three of the questions. For a fun twist for younger children, see if you can answer some of the questions about one of your children's close friends whom you don't really know.

• **How do you know you have a relationship with someone?**
• **What do you think a relationship is?**

Share: When we're in a relationship with others, we spend time together, show our love for each other, support each other, encourage each other, and things like this. These are things we do as a family, and things we do with our close friends. We can explore how to do this with God.

Activity 2: God's Treasure

Point: Reading God's Word is one way to get to know God.

Supplies: Before your family time, hide a Bible in your home. Then write clues that will eventually lead family members to the Bible.

Share: There's a treasure hidden in our home. It's up to you to find it!

Activity: Give children the first clue, and follow along as they search for the hidden treasure. When they find the Bible, congratulate them on their brilliant detective skills, then gather again for discussion.

Discuss these questions:
- **Do you think most people think of the Bible as a treasure? Why or why not?**
- **What do you think makes the Bible a treasure?** (Possible answers: It has wisdom in it; it tells us how to know God; it tells us about Jesus; it tells us about others.)
- **What kind of riches does the Bible bring us?**

Share: The Bible doesn't lead us to money or other things most people think of as treasure. But by reading the Bible we get to know God better. The Bible tells us *about* God, and tells us how to *know* God too.

Ask: **What treasures have you already gotten from the Bible?**

The answers to this question will vary depending on the ages and spiritual maturity of your children. They might suggest some of these answers:
- **Knowing about God's love**
- **Learning how God wants us to treat others**
- **Gaining courage for hard or scary times**
- **Finding out about Jesus and what He did for me**
- **Learning about other people who had troubles and how God helped them**

Share: Reading the Bible every day, or even a few times a week, can help us get to know God better. The more we read, the more treasure we find! There are verses in the Bible that tell us more about how to get to know God better.

 Read the following verses, discussing the questions after each reference:

1 John 4:7-12
- **What do these verses tell us about knowing God?** (We must show love to know God; if we don't love others, we don't know God.)
- **What actions has God taken toward us?** (He sent Jesus; He let Jesus be a sacrifice for us.)
- **What do we know about God because of these actions?** (He loves us a lot! Showing love to others is very important to God.)
- **If we're friends of God, how should we act?** (We should love others.)

Share: We learn from these verses that God is love, and He loves us so much that He sent His Son to die for us. Now that's a real friend! But these verses also tell us that the more we show love to others, the more we get to know God!

James 4:8

- **What does this verse tell us about getting to know God?** (If we get near to Him, He will get near to us.)
- **How do we get near God?** (We purify our hearts; we ask God to forgive our sins.)
- **Think about friends you have and how you got to be close to them. What made your friendship stronger?**

Share: When we want to get to know someone better, we spend time with that person. The same is true with God. If we want to get to know God better, we need to spend more time with Him. What do you think this means? (Possible answers are reading the Bible, going to church, and praying.)

Share: Doing these things is a way of "hanging out" with God! The more time you spend with God, the more you get to know God.

These are just examples of the treasures we find in the Bible. The more we read the Bible, the more we get to know God.

Activity 3: Who Said That?

Point: The more we know God, the more we know God's voice.

 Supplies: You'll need a Bible.

Consider these questions:
- **Is it hard for you to tell which family member is talking when your eyes are closed? Why or why not?**
- **Do you have friends whose voices you know so well that you know who's calling when you hear their voices on the phone? How can you tell who's who?**

Age Adjustments

Let the ages of your children determine the difficulty of the clues you give. For example, A Young Child might determine that "The mail carrier stops here every day" will lead her to your mailbox for the next clue, while AN OLDER CHILD might be lead to the same destination by the clue "No one visits me on Sundays."

OLDER CHILDREN may enjoy the added challenge of having Bible references for all the clues. For example, the clue Philemon 22 would lead to the guest room, while Isaiah 30:24 could lead to the tool shed or the silverware drawer. Use a concordance to help you locate verses naming places or objects such as these.

Make this activity fun for ALL YOUR FAMILY MEMBERS by insisting that all family members be together when each clue is read, and by letting children take turns looking for or reading the next clue. Be sure each child gets a turn, not just the children who can run to the next clue fastest.

- Do you think you'd be more likely to follow the voice of a friend or family member, or the voice of a stranger? Explain your answer.
- Have you ever been afraid, then heard the voice of a friend or family member on the phone, or in the dark or something, and then been comforted? If so, tell about that time.

Let everyone open their eyes, then share: We've spent so much time together that we almost always recognize the voices of others in our family. The voices of those we love bring us comfort and we can trust these voices for guidance. The Bible explains that it can be the same way for us with God.

 Read John 10:1-6, then discuss:
- Do you think you could recognize the voice of God?
- Do you think you can tell when you hear a voice that's not from God?
- What things do you know God would never tell you to do?

Share: When someone encourages us to lie, cheat, steal, be mean to others, or do anything we know is wrong, we can be sure that's not the voice of God!
- What things do you think God might tell you that you should do?

Share: When someone encourages us to be respectful, show love, be kind, be patient, use loving words, or do anything we know is right, that might be God speaking to us!

WRAP-UP

Gather everyone in a circle and have family members take turns answering this question: **What's one thing you've learned about God today?**

Next, tell kids you've got a new "Life Slogan" you'd like to share with them.

Life Slogan: Today's Life Slogan is this: "To love Him is to know Him!"
Have family members repeat the slogan two or three times to help them learn it. Then encourage them to practice saying it during the week so they can talk about it at your next family night session.

Close in Prayer: Allow time for each family member to share prayer concerns and answers to prayer. Then close your time together with prayer for each concern. Thank God for listening to and caring about us.

Remember to record prayer requests so you can refer to them in the future as you see God answering them.

Additional Resources:

Night Light Tales by Andy Holmes (ages 4–8)
Wings of an Angel by Sigmund Brouwer (ages 8–12)
Family Bible Challenge CD ROM (ages 6–adult) ChariotMedia
Bible Challenge Game (ages 12–up) Rainfall
Bible Quizmasters (ages 4–6) Rainfall

QUESTIONNAIRE

Answer these questions about yourself.

1. What makes you mad?

2. What's your favorite thing to eat for breakfast?

3. What makes you happy?

4. Who is your best friend?

5. What is your favorite thing to do in your spare time?

6. What makes you feel sad?

7. What do others miss about you when you're gone?

⊚ 4: Jars of Clay

Exploring how God controls our lives

Scripture
- Isaiah 45:9 and 64:8—God is the potter, we are the clay.
- Psalm 139:13—God created each of us.
- James 1:2-4—God allows testing to help us mature.

ACTIVITY OVERVIEW		
Activity	Summary	Pre-Session Prep
Activity 1: Out of Control!	Enjoy as family members take turns controlling each other's actions.	You'll need blindfolds.
Activity 2: What Are You Making?	Compare God's control of our lives to a potter's control of clay.	You'll need (1) a video showing a potter working with clay, and (2) a Bible.
Activity 3: Into the Fire	Discover reasons for testing in life.	You'll need a Bible.

Main Points:

— Some things in life are out of our control.

— God is like a potter, controlling and shaping us.

— God shapes us through testing.

LIFE SLOGAN: "God is the potter of the clay. I am being formed His way."

Make it your own
In the space provided below, outline the flow and add any additional ideas to guide you through the process of conducting this family night.

Prayer & Praise Items
In the space provided below, list any items you wish to pray about or give praise for during this family night session.

Journal
In the space provided below, capture a record of what fun or meaningful things which happened during this family night session.

WARM-UP

Open with Prayer: Begin by having a family member pray, asking God to help everyone in the family understand more about Him through this time. After prayer, review your last lesson by asking these questions:

• **What fun activity do you remember from our last lesson?**
• **What did you learn from that fun activity?**
• **What was the Life Slogan?**

Share: There are times when life is out of our control. Let's see why God allows these situations, and how we should respond.

ACTIVITY 1: Out of Control!

Point: Some things in life are out of our control.

Supplies: You'll need blindfolds (bandannas, dish towels, or pillowcases work great).

Activity: Take family members to a park or other open and safe setting. (There shouldn't be cars or dangerous things such as open pits.) If you like, take time to play on the equipment, toss a Frisbee or football, or have a picnic.

When you're ready to begin, gather family members and form pairs. (If you have an uneven number of people, it's okay to have one trio.) Distribute blindfolds and have one person in each pair put one on. (Be sure to include yourself in this activity!) When everyone's ready, explain that the seeing partner should lead the blindfolded partner around the park.

This might include sitting on a swing, ducking under the monkey bars, or dodging a tree branch. It will be up to the seeing partner to ensure that the blindfolded partner doesn't become injured.

After several minutes of wandering about the park, call family members together again and allow blindfolds to be removed. Then have partners switch places, so that the former seeing partner is now the blindfolded partner. Repeat the exercise so everyone has a chance to be blindfolded.

Again call everyone together. Gather the blindfolds and return home. On the way, or as soon as you get home, discuss these questions:

- **Which was better, being the blindfolded person or the seeing person? Explain your reasons.**
- **How would this activity have been easier if we did it in our own home?**
- **What were the good and bad points of being the seeing person?**
- **What were the good and bad points of being the blindfolded person?**

Share: Most of us don't like the feeling of being out of control. We like to see where we're going so we can watch out for rocks that might trip us or branches that might slap us in the face. Besides seeing where you're going, what are other areas of your life where you like to be in control?

Family members might think of being in control of their own bedtimes; of their allowances, their chores, or other responsibilities; of choosing their friends; and so on.

Ask these questions:
- **What are times when you can't be in control?**

Answers will vary, but could include times when we're sick, times when parents or others in authority make decisions for us (such as bedtimes, speed limits, when recess is over, or what time someone must be at work), or times when situations are simply beyond our control (such as when a loved one dies or when a person gets laid off from a job).

- **How do you feel about times when you can't be in control?**

Share: For some people, being out of control is frustrating. Others don't mind letting others take control for them. But we can always take comfort in knowing that God is ultimately in control of our lives.

ACTIVITY 2: What Are You Making?

Point: God is like a potter, controlling and shaping us.

 Supplies: You'll need a Bible and a video of a potter forming clay on a potter's wheel. (Check your local library or a craft shop with instructional videos.) If necessary, use play dough to demonstrate the potter/clay process yourself.

Activity: Show your family the process of a potter creating something from clay. After watching for several minutes, pause and ask these questions:

- **What do you notice about the potter?** (The potter is skillful, knows what he or she is doing, has an idea in mind as to what the clay will become, plans to make something useful from the clay.)
- **What do you notice about the clay?** (It doesn't resist what the potter does; it can be molded or shaped again and again until it's in the form the potter wants.)
- **What is the clay saying to the potter?** (Nothing!)

Share: The Bible compares us to clay.

 Read Isaiah 45:9 and 64:8 aloud, then discuss these questions:

- **According to these verses, how is God like a potter?** (He created us like a potter creates from clay; God knows what He's doing with us just like a potter knows what he's doing with clay.)
- **How are we like clay?** (We're molded by God; we're the product of His hands.)
- **How are we unlike the clay?** (We complain and the clay doesn't; we want to know what God's making out of us before He's done; we try to get out of God's control.)

Share: God is like a potter. Even when we feel like our lives are out of control, He's shaping us into an image He has in mind so He can use us for His work. The Bible tells us God made us.

Read Psalm 139:13 aloud.

Share: Just like a potter might make each pot special by putting a handle on one pot, or a spout on another, God made each of us to be used in a special way. And just like a potter knows what's best for making a pot, so God knows what's best for making us.

Age Adjustments

YOUNGER CHILDREN may not appreciate the finer points of a pottery-making demonstration. Instead, give them some clay and join them in making teacups or bowls. Discuss how moldable the clay is, and compare this to the way God molds us and shapes us according to His plans.

OLDER CHILDREN might like visiting a factory where stoneware, pottery, or china is made. See if there are any factories of this sort near you. Otherwise, you might arrange to view a potter's demonstration at a craft show. If your kids are really interested, consider enrolling the whole family in a pottery-making class.

Take a moment here to point out one special "feature" God has made in each family member, such as a bright smile, a generous spirit, or a sharp mind. Be sure each of these features is positive as you take time to affirm the specialness of each family member.

ACTIVITY 3: Into the Fire

Point: God shapes us through testing.

 Supplies: You'll need a Bible.

Activity: If your pottery video explains further steps to the creation of a finished product, watch the rest of it to understand how many different steps a bit of clay must go through before being finished.

Share: There are many steps to creating a beautiful piece of pottery or china. The clay must be rolled, squeezed, and patted. It's spun around and around on the potter's wheel. Then it's put into a hot oven, then painted or glazed, then put back into the oven. If any of these steps are left out, the pot might crack, crumble, collapse, or otherwise be ugly and useless. It's a long process, but in the end a lump of clay has become a beautiful and useful object. If the clay had feelings, it probably would complain about the whole process.

God, as the potter, is taking us, lumps of clay, and forming us into something useful and beautiful. But along the way we must go through stretching, molding, and other situations just like the clay.

Discuss these questions:
- **Why do you think God allows us to go through hard times?** (To test us; to help us grow; to make us stronger.)
- **What's a hard time you've gone through recently?** (This

might be anything from a long illness or loss of job to a difficult test or unhappy situation with friends.)
- **What have you learned from this situation?**

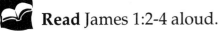 **Read** James 1:2-4 aloud.
- **What kind of attitude does God want us to have when we're going through these hard times that are out of our control?** (An attitude of joy.)
- **What does God want to accomplish through these hard times?** (God wants to test our faith in Him; He wants to develop perseverance in our lives; He wants us to be mature, complete, and not lacking in anything.)

Share: Just as the pot will crumble under pressure if it's not properly molded, stretched, and heated, so we'll crumble under the stress of life unless God uses different methods to make us stronger. As we learn how God cares for us through the times when life seems out of control, we grow and become stronger in our relationship with God and more like Jesus.

WRAP-UP

Gather everyone in a circle and have family members take turns answering this question: **What's one thing you've learned about God today?**

Next, tell kids you've got a new "Life Slogan" you'd like to share with them.

Life Slogan: Today's Life Slogan is this: "God is the potter of the clay. I am being formed His way!" Have family members repeat the slogan two or three times to help them learn it. Then encourage them to practice saying it during the week so they can talk about it at your next family night session.

Age Adjustments

YOUNGER CHILDREN might not understand the abstract concepts of testing. Simply reassure them that just as parents want what's best for their children, so God wants what's best for us. Children don't always understand why their parents set rules, punish them, or make them try new things. But parents know that doing these things help make the child a stronger and better person. In the same way, God is in control of our lives even when we don't understand why certain things are happening.

OLDER CHILDREN might want to explore Bible characters who went through various tests and compare how these men and women became stronger and more useful to God. Consider the lives of Abraham, Moses, David, Ruth, Esther, Paul, or any of the 12 disciples.

If you or a friend have a copy of the Wayne Watson recording "Touch of Master's Hand," play it because this song shares a message similar to this lesson. School-aged Children and Older will be able to understand this message and discuss how it relates to the lesson.

Close in Prayer: Allow time for each family member to share prayer concerns and answers to prayer. Then close your time together with prayer for each concern. Thank God for listening to and caring about us.

Remember to record your prayer requests so you can refer to them in the future as you see God answering them.

Additional Resources:

The King without a Shadow by R.C. Sproul (ages 4–8)
The Hair-Pulling Bear Dog by Lee Roddy (ages 8–12)
Kid's Choices Game (ages 6–12) Rainfall

@ 5: God Cares for Me

Exploring God's love and care for His children

Scripture:

• Genesis 6:5-22—God tells Noah to build an ark.
• Genesis 8:1-12—The animals go on the ark and the earth is flooded.
• Genesis 8:13-21 and 9:8-17—God's covenant with Noah.

ACTIVITY OVERVIEW		
Activity	Summary	Pre-Session Prep
Activity 1: Construction Zone	Build a smaller version of Noah's ark.	You'll need a large box, tape, crayons, a knife, stuffed animals, a doll, and a Bible.
Activity 2: Floating Safari	Relive life on the ark.	Continue with the supplies from the previous activity.
Activity 3: The Meaning of Rainbows	Discover the real reason for rainbows.	You'll need a Bible, paper, and markers or crayons.

Main Points:

—God loved and cared for Noah and his family.
—God also took care of the animals.
—God loves and cares about you.

LIFE SLOGAN: "Noah was safe from rain and sea. God cared for him, God cares for me!"

Make it your own

In the space provided below, outline the flow and add any additional ideas to guide you through the process of conducting this family night.

Prayer & Praise Items

In the space provided below, list any items you wish to pray about or give praise for during this family night session.

Journal

In the space provided below, capture a record of what fun or meaningful things which happened during this family night session.

Session Tip

We intentionally have provided more material than we would expect to be used in a single "Family Night" session. You know your family's unique interests and life circumstances best, so feel free to adapt this session to meet your family members' needs. Remember, short and simple is better than long and comprehensive.

WARM-UP

Open with Prayer: Begin by having a family member pray, asking God to help everyone in the family understand more about Him through this time. After prayer, review your last lesson by asking these questions:
- **What do you remember from our last lesson?**
- **Do you remember the Life Slogan?**
- **How have your actions changed because of things we've been learning recently?**

Share: We're going to learn about how much God loves us from the example of a man named Noah.

ACTIVITY 1: Construction Zone

Point: God loved and cared for Noah and his family.

Supplies: You'll need a large box, such as a refrigerator box or a wardrobe box from a moving company, heavy tape, stuffed animals, a doll, a knife, and markers or crayons. One of the stuffed animals should be a bird of some kind. You'll also need a Bible or a children's story-book with the story of Noah in it.

Note: As the Bible account of Noah's story is very long, we suggest you read it yourself ahead of time, then retell the story in your own words, using the Bible as a reference to remind you of the main events in the story. Or use a children's Bible storybook.

Activity: Before your family time, hide stuffed animals around your home. If you don't have many stuffed animals, cut animal shapes out of construction paper and hide these. Or you could cut out pictures of animals from magazines, mount these on heavier paper, and hide them. Be sure to include a bird.

Place a doll that could be Noah inside the large box and tape the box securely shut. Again, if you don't have an appropriate doll (a Ken doll, a GI Joe, or other male action figure), cut a figure from heavy paper and draw on features such as a face and clothing.

When all is ready, bring your family members into the room. Don't explain what the box is or what's in it. Just leave it in the center of the room as you begin.

Age Adjustments

Take OLDER CHILDREN to a park or other open setting and measure off the dimensions of the ark. Use yarn or string to draw an outline of how big the ark would be using the dimensions given in the Bible. See if you can measure a building, tree, or other tall object to see how tall the ark was. Stand inside this area and imagine what it must have been like to have had so many animals, people, food, and so forth on a ship of this size.

Share: I want to read you a story from the Bible about a man named Noah.

Read the account of Noah from Genesis 6:5-22. This tells of God's grief over the sin of humanity and His command to Noah to build the ark. If you're reading from a children's storybook, read only this far in the story.

Share: God was very sad at how evil people had become. The only person left on earth who loved God was Noah. So even though God was going to destroy all the people on the earth, He cared about Noah and wanted Noah to be safe. Now let's use this box to make our own ark!

Bring out the markers or crayons and let children draw and color boards, windows, decks, and other features of the ark. Have an adult use a sharp knife or scissors to cut a few windows and an opening large enough for the stuffed animals and family members to crawl through. At this point the children will discover "Noah"!

When the building of the ark is complete, stand back to admire the work.

Share: God wanted to clean the world of wickedness, but because He loved Noah, God took care of him.

ACTIVITY 2: Floating Safari

Point: God also took care of the animals.

 Supplies: You'll need a Bible or the storybook you're already using, plus the animals you've already hidden.

📖 **Read** the next portion of the story, from Genesis 7:1-24. If you're reading from a storybook, read the portion where Noah and his family and all the animals enter the ark and the rains begin.

Share: Noah had all those animals on the ark. We'd better find some animals to put on this ark.

Send your children off to find the hidden stuffed animals. As they retrieve them, have them place the animals into the box. When all the animals (including the bird) are on board, explain that Noah and all his family had to get in with the animals, so you'd all better get in as well.

If your box is big enough, cram everyone in the family into the box except one adult. If it's not large enough, have only the children squeeze in among the stuffed animals.

While in the box, rock back and forth to pretend you're riding the waves. The adult outside the box can tap on the box to make the sound of rain or thunder, and gently rock the children inside the box.

While you're doing this, talk about what it must have been like for Noah and his family to be on that ark with all those animals. What did it smell like? How did they take care of the animals?

Have each family member think of a favorite animal, then let everyone loudly make the noise of their chosen animal for one minute. How did Noah and his family live with all that noise?

Finally, pretend that the rain has stopped. With everyone still in the ark, have the adult outside the ark continue reading the account from the Bible or storybook.

📖 **Read** Genesis 8:1-12, or the portion of your storybook telling of the bird being sent out to look for dry land.

Have one of the children hold the stuffed bird out a window. The adult outside can take the bird and "fly" it around looking for a twig. Discuss what it meant for the bird to first find no place to land, then to bring back a twig, then

Age Adjustments

CHILDREN OF ALL AGES will get a better appreciation for this Bible story if you visit a zoo near the time of this lesson. Think about how big those elephants are, how tall the giraffes are, and how prickly the porcupines are! How did these animals all get into the ark? What was it like with so many different kinds of animals? How would you have felt being so close to these animals for such a long time?

for the bird to not return. (The water hadn't gone down enough to find a place to land, then it had gone down enough to find a tree, then it finally went down far enough that the bird didn't have to return to the ark anymore.)

ACTIVITY 3: The Meaning of Rainbows

Point: God loves and cares about you.

Supplies: You'll need a Bible, paper, and crayons or markers.

Share: Finally, the land was dry and Noah and the animals could get off the ark.

Activity: Have everyone get out of your box ark, then read Genesis 8:13-21 and 9:8-17. If you're reading in a Bible storybook, complete the story, including God's placement of the rainbow in the sky. Consider these questions:

• **What have you learned about God from this story?** (God loved Noah and took care of him; wicked people make God sad; God cares about animals too; God loves us and won't ever make another flood to destroy all people.)
• **Why did God make rainbows?** (To remind Himself and us of His promise to never destroy all life in a flood again.)

Share: Let's draw pictures of rainbows to remind us that God keeps His promises.

Age Adjustments

OLDER CHILDREN may be interested in learning more about recent archaeological searches for Noah's ark. There are a variety of books and video tapes on the subject at Christian bookstores.

Use paper and crayons or markers to draw colorful rainbows. Have each person place his or her rainbow where it can be seen every day for the next week.

Share: Every time you see your rainbow, or one that another family member has drawn, think about how much God loves you and how He takes care of you!

WRAP-UP

Gather everyone in a circle and have family members take turns answering this question: **What's one thing you've learned about God today?**

Next, tell kids you've got a new "Life Slogan" you'd like to share with them.

Life Slogan: Today's Life Slogan is this: **"Noah was safe from rain and sea. God cared for him, God cares for me!"** Have family members repeat the slogan two or three times to help them learn it. Then encourage them to practice saying it during the week so they can talk about it at your next family night session.

Close in Prayer: Allow time for each family member to share prayer concerns and answers to prayer. Then close your time together with prayer for each concern. Thank God for listening to and caring about us.

Remember to record your prayer requests so you can refer to them in the future as you see God answering them.

Additional Resources:

A First Look at God (ages 4–8)
Jesus Loves Little Children (ages 1–3)
Peel & Play Noah and the Ark (ages 3–8) Rainfall
Noah & Ark Playset (ages 5–10) Rainfall
S.S. Ark Bath Toy (ages 6 months to 3)

6: Chain Reaction

Exploring the consequences of sin

Scripture:
- Romans 6:23—The consequence of sin is death.
- 1 John 1:9—God forgives those who confess their sins.
- Galatians 6:7—We reap what we sow.

ACTIVITY OVERVIEW		
Activity	**Summary**	**Pre-Session Prep**
Activity 1: Down, Down, Dominoes	Learn about chain reactions.	You'll need dominoes.
Activity 2: I Confess	Understand the power of forgiveness.	You'll need paper with "GOD" written on it, tape, and a Bible.
Activity 3: Permanent Reaction	Discover the physical consequences of sin.	You'll need a candy bar and a Bible.

Main Points:

—Every action has a reaction.

—When we confess, God forgives us for sinning.

—Even though we're forgiven, we have to live with the consequences of our sins.

LIFE SLOGAN: "Sin with confession serves as a lesson."

Make it your own
In the space provided below, outline the flow and add any additional ideas to guide you through the process of conducting this family night.

Prayer & Praise Items
In the space provided below, list any items you wish to pray about or give praise for during this family night session.

Journal
In the space provided below, capture a record of what fun or meaningful things which happened during this family night session.

Session Tip

We intentionally have provided more material than we would expect to be used in a single "Family Night" session. You know your family's unique interests and life circumstances best, so feel free to adapt this session to meet your family members' needs. Remember, short and simple is better than long and comprehensive.

WARM-UP

Open with Prayer: Begin by having a family member pray, asking God to help everyone in the family understand more about Him through this time. After prayer, review your last lesson by asking these questions:

- **What was something you thought was interesting from our last lesson?**
- **What was the Life Slogan?**
- **What does the Life Slogan mean?**

Share: Today we'll be learning more about what happens when we sin.

ACTIVITY 1: Down, Down, Dominoes

Point: Every action has a reaction.

 Supplies: You'll need a box of wooden or plastic dominoes.

Activity: Have family members work together balancing dominoes on their ends in a line. Place them so that when one is bumped or knocked over, the others will follow in a chain reaction. See how long and complicated you can make these lines of dominoes before one falls over and knocks down the rest. Can you make the line split into two or three lines? Can you get the line to go up a ramp or slope? Can you make letters of the alphabet or spell the names of family members?

When you've had fun with the dominoes, put them away and gather for discussion:

• What was fun about this activity?
• What was frustrating about it?
• If you knock one over, it knocks down all the others in the line after it. Is there any way to stop this?

Age Adjustments

OLDER KIDS might have fun inventing "Rube Goldbergs," or contraptions in which one action sets off a string of reactions. For example, a pulled string releases a hammer that falls on a clothespin that releases a toy car that speeds down a track and bumps into a lever that flips a switch to make the lights come on. Look for children's physics books at the library for examples of how to make these wacky "machines."

The same idea, only easier for parents, is followed in the board game "Mousetrap." If you have, or can borrow, this game, it's another great example of a chain reaction and how one action can set off a string of reactions. Sure, it's a hassle to set up, but it's a lot of fun!

Share: No matter how loud you yell, or how frustrated you feel, when the dominoes start going down, there's no way to stop them. This is called a chain reaction. When one things is set off, other reactions begin that can't be stopped.

• Does this remind you of any situations in real life?

Answers to this will vary, but might include:

• If you poke a balloon with a pin, it pops and cannot be refilled with air.
• If you stay up late at night, it's hard to wake up early the next morning.
• If you hit your thumb with a hammer, it will hurt.
• If you give someone a hug, you'll both feel better.
• If you do your chores, you'll earn your allowance.

Together think of as many different action/reaction combinations as possible. You might think of longer ones as well, such as this one: (1) Dad thinks of how much he loves Mom; (2) Dad stops and buys a flower for Mom; (3) Mom's so happy, she makes a big pie for dinner; (4) everyone loves the pie and Mom and Dad's happiness, so they feel happy too!

Share: Even the most simple action always causes a reaction of some kind. This reaction can be called a consequence. Let's explore more about how actions and their consequences relate to our lives.

ACTIVITY 2: I Confess

Point: When we confess, God forgives us for sinning.

Supplies: You'll need a sheet of paper with "GOD" written on it, tape, and a Bible.

Share: One example of an action that causes a reaction is sin. When we sin, there's a reaction, or consequence. We can demonstrate that with a little game.

Activity: On one wall of the room, tape a sheet of paper with "GOD" written on it. Have everyone stand next to this sign.

Share: When we're without sin, we're close to God. Now let's think of wrong actions, which are sins.

Have family members take turns naming sins. This doesn't have to be a time of confession, but instead a time of thinking about what wrong things we're likely to do. Also, be sure to include sins common among family members. Someone is sure to say "murder" right away, but it's highly unlikely anyone in your family will commit this sin. Encourage family members to think of things they really struggle with doing, such as teasing a sibling, lying about "who started it," stealing change from Mom's purse, cheating on a spelling test, gossiping about a friend, and so on.

As each person names a sin, have that person move one step back from the God sign. Continue naming sins and moving away from God.

When everyone is far away from the God sign, share: The Bible says the wages of sin is death (Romans 6:23). That means that the reaction, or consequence, of our actions is death.

Share: God doesn't "rank" sin, saying that one sin is worse than another. All sins have the consequence of death. Now we're far from God and have the consequence of death to look forward to. What are we going to do?

 Read 1 John 1:9 aloud and question:
- **What does this verse say we need to do?** (Confess our sins.)
- **What does confess mean?** (To admit doing something wrong; to tell of what you've done.)
- **What is the reaction to the action of confessing?** (We're forgiven and purified.)

Take a few moments for each person to ask God to forgive his or her sins. Again, this doesn't have to be a long, drawn-out confessional, but rather a simple time of asking God to forgive us for what we've done wrong. After everyone has prayed, have family members move back to the God sign.

Share: The consequence of confession is forgiveness. This means we can be close to God again. But there's another reaction or consequence to sin we haven't yet discussed.

ACTIVITY 3: Permanent Reaction

Point: Even though we're forgiven, we have to live with the consequences of our sins.

Supplies: You'll need a candy bar and a Bible. Before the family time, prepare by having another family member read through the skit's script with you.

Activity: Put on a little skit for your family. Before your family time, ask your spouse or another family member to help you with this skit. You'll need a candy bar for the skit. Fill your names into the appropriate places.

THE CANDY BAR

Scene: Carla and Reggie are sitting next to each other. Carla has a candy bar in her hand.

CARLA: I need to go wash my hands before I have this candy bar. Will you keep an eye on it for me?

REGGIE: Sure!

CARLA: You won't eat it, will you?

REGGIE: Of course not! I'll keep it safely here for you.

[Carla hands Reggie the candy bar and goes into the bathroom to wash her hands. Reggie watches until she's gone, then quickly opens the candy bar and eats it as fast as he can. When Carla returns, Reggie acts like nothing happened.]

CARLA: Where's my candy bar?

REGGIE: What candy bar?

CARLA: The one I asked you to watch for me!

REGGIE: I, uha dog ate it!

CARLA: That's not true, Reggie. Tell me the truth. Did you eat my candy bar?

REGGIE: *[sadly]* Yes, I confess. I ate your candy bar. I'm sorry. Will you forgive me?

CARLA: I forgive you.

[Reggie and Carla hug.]

When everyone has given you a big round of applause, you might want to hand out candy bars to the rest of the family.

Share: It seems like this story has a happy ending. Reggie sinned but Carla forgave him. But there's one problem. Does anyone know what it is?

Carla still doesn't have a candy bar! Even though she was willing to forgive Reggie, there is another consequence to his action, and that's that the candy bar is gone. Sometimes we sin and are forgiven, but there's still another consequence for our actions. What are other examples of this in real life?

Answers could include:

- A student admits to cheating on a test and is forgiven, but still fails the test.
- Brother and sister fight over the remote control. When they're sorry, Mom forgives them and they forgive each other. But they're punished by not being allowed to watch television for a week.
- An unmarried couple has sexual relations. If they confess, God will forgive them, but they can never regain their virginity, and they may have to live with the consequence of pregnancy.
- An employee steals money from the boss. God will forgive the employee, but the employee still will have to live with the consequence of losing his job, and may even have the consequence of going to jail.

Share: God will always forgive us if we ask Him to, so the consequence of death and being far from God is removed. But we still have to live with the earthly consequences of our actions.

 Read Galatians 6:7 and discuss:

Age Adjustments

This is a good time to discuss appropriate punishments or consequences with OLDER CHILDREN AND TEENAGERS. As children look forward to increased freedoms as they get older, they need to understand the increased responsibilities and the consequences of failure. This might include using the family car, dating, holding a job, and other privileges. When these privileges are abused, there are consequences. Some of these consequences can be extremely difficult, such as car accidents or teen pregnancy.

• **What does this verse mean?** (We have to live with the consequences of our actions.)

Share: If we sin, we know God will forgive us. But we still will have to live with the consequences of our actions. That's why we need to think about our actions before we do them! We can save ourselves, others, and God a lot of pain if we think about the reactions that will be caused by our actions.

WRAP-UP

Gather everyone in a circle and have family members take turns answering this question: What's one thing you've learned about God today?

Next, tell kids you've got a new "Life Slogan" you'd like to share with them.

Life Slogan: Today's Life Slogan is this: "Sin with confession serves as a lesson!" Have family members repeat the slogan two or three times to help them learn it. Then encourage them to practice saying it during the week so they can talk about it at your next family night session.

Close in Prayer: Allow time for each family member to share prayer concerns and answers to prayer. Then close your time together with prayer for each concern. Thank God for listening to and caring about us.

Remember to record your prayer requests so you can refer to them in the future as you see God answering them.

Additional Resources:

The Children's Discovery Bible (ages 4–8)

⊚ 7: Personal Message

Exploring why Jesus was born as a human

Scripture:
- John 1:14—Jesus became human.
- John 1:18—We see God through seeing Jesus.
- John 8:19—If we know Jesus, we know the Father.
- John 12:49-50—God gave Jesus a message for us.

ACTIVITY OVERVIEW		
Activity	Summary	Pre-Session Prep
Activity 1: Talk to Me!	Learn how we communicate in a variety of ways.	You'll need no supplies.
Activity 2: Glub, Buzz, and Bark!	Discover that we communicate best with those who, like us, are humans.	You'll need a goldfish in water and a Bible.
Activity 3: The Sparrows	Share a story relating the importance of Jesus becoming human.	You'll need a Bible.

Main Points:

—Humans can communicate with each other.

—Jesus came as a human so we could understand God's message.

—It's important that we listen to Jesus' message.

LIFE SLOGAN: "Born on Christmas Day, God showed us the way!"

Make it your own
In the space provided below, outline the flow and add any additional ideas to guide you through the process of conducting this family night.

Prayer & Praise Items
In the space provided below, list any items you wish to pray about or give praise for during this family night session.

Journal
In the space provided below, capture a record of what fun or meaningful things which happened during this family night session.

Session Tip

We intentionally have provided more material than we would expect to be used in a single "Family Night" session. You know your family's unique interests and life circumstances best, so feel free to adapt this session to meet your family members' needs. Remember, short and simple is better than long and comprehensive.

WARM-UP

Open with Prayer: Begin by having a family member pray, asking God to help everyone in the family understand more about Him through this time. After prayer, review your last lesson by asking these questions:

- **What do you remember from our last lesson?**
- **Do you remember the Life Slogan?**
- **What was something fun about our last lesson?**

Share: Today we're going to answer the question "Why did God send Jesus as a baby?"

ACTIVITY 1: Talk to Me!

Point: Humans can communicate with each other.

 Supplies: Supplies will vary according to what each family member chooses to teach. You won't need to gather anything before the lesson.

Activity: Explain that each family member will have the opportunity to teach everyone else how to do something. Allow some time for everyone to think about what they could teach others to do. Ideas can be silly or serious, short or long. It can be something everyone actually already knows how to do, or a new thing only you know how to do. If anyone gets stuck on what to do, here are a few suggestions.

Teach others how to:
- tie shoes
- do a somersault
- make chocolate milk
- play a song on the piano (or other instrument)
- gargle
- inflate a balloon
- do a basic stitch in knitting, crochet, or needlepoint

Note: Suggest that family members choose activities they think everyone will realistically be able to do. For example, your 16-year-old may want to teach everyone how to drive, but this is something your 7-year-old won't be able to do.

When everyone has decided what lesson they'll teach, ask if anyone would like to volunteer to teach their "skill" without speaking. Motions would still be allowed, but no words could be spoken. If no one volunteers, offer to do this yourself. (It's also okay if *everyone* volunteers!)

Take turns teaching each other your special skills until everyone in the family can at least make a good attempt at what you've taught. Be sure those who've volunteered to teach in silence follow through (although laughter certainly *is* allowed). Have fun!

When all lessons have been taught, gather together to discuss:

- **Did you have any difficulty in teaching others what you wanted them to do? If so, explain.**
- **What made not being able to talk a challenge for the teacher? What made it a challenge for the learners?**
- **What strengths do you have in communicating to others?** (Possible answers could be facial expressions, a good sense of humor, strong writing skills, a large vocabulary, and so on.)
- **Do you think you'd be able to communicate a few basic messages to someone who spoke a different language? How would you do that?**

Share: Even when we don't share the same language or are kept from using our voices, we're able to communicate a message to others. This is part of being human. God made us so that we can talk to each other, write messages to each other, express ourselves with our hands, faces, or other movements, and so on.

ACTIVITY 2: Glub, Buzz, and Bark!

Point: Jesus came as a human so we could understand God's message.

 Supplies: You'll need (1) a goldfish in water and (2) a Bible. A bug in a jar could also be used in place of a fish.

Activity: Bring out the goldfish and place it where everyone can see it.

Share: Now I'd like us all to teach this goldfish the same lessons we taught each other.

Most family members will laugh or complain that this can't be done. A young child may want to try, and this is fine. But after a few minutes it will be obvious that the fish isn't understanding the lesson.

Consider these questions:

- **Is there any way to make this fish understand us? Would talking work? writing a note? playing music?**
- **If you wanted to tell this fish that a cat was around that corner and he'd better hide, how would you do this?**

Share: Since we're humans, there's really no way for us to make a fish understand us. But if we were to become a fish ourselves, we could communicate to the fish in whatever way fishes communicate.

- **How does this example of the fish help us understand why Jesus came as a human?** (We couldn't talk to God; God wanted to give us a message; we couldn't get to know God unless He made a way for us to understand His "language.")

Share: The Bible tells us about God becoming a man.

 Read John 1:14 and 18, John 8:19, and John 12:49-50.

Question: What do these verses tell us about Jesus? (Jesus became a human and lived on the earth; people saw Jesus in real life; we can't see God, but God made Himself known through Jesus; if we know Jesus, we know God; Jesus gave us God's message, which leads us to eternal life.)

Share: God loved us so much that He was willing to become a man, Jesus, so we could know about God's love for us!

Age Adjustments

OLDER CHILDREN may enjoy discussing methods humans have undertaken to attempt communicating to animals. Books or videos from the library might help in this discussion of how people have taught monkeys sign language or mimicked the whistles of dolphins and whales.

During your discussion, ask: Do you think humans and animals are really able to communicate? Why or why not? Do you think dogs, cats, rabbits, or other pets can understand you? Explain your answer.

Point out that while we may be able to communicate simple messages or commands to animals, it's obvious that the *best* way to communicate with them would be to become one of these animals ourselves. In the same way, God communicates with us in simple ways like letting us know He exists through the majesty of creation. But to let us know the message of His love for us, God chose the *best* way to communicate—He sent Jesus as a human.

ACTIVITY 3: The Sparrows

Point: It's important that we listen to Jesus' message.

Supplies: You'll need a Bible.

Share: There's a story of a man who didn't believe in Jesus. He thought the whole idea of God sending His Son as a man was foolish. Even though his wife and children tried to make him understand, this man refused to believe in Jesus.

One night when his wife and children were away, a huge snowstorm blew in. As the man looked out his window, he saw a group of sparrows huddling on the branches outside.

"Those birds will freeze to death in this blizzard!" the man said.

He put on his coat, ran outside, and opened the barn door. *This will be a place they can be safe and warm,* he thought to himself.

But there was one problem. The birds didn't know that the barn would keep them safe. The man tried shooing them into the open door, but they only fluttered around and settled again on the barren tree branches. Again and again the man tried to get the birds into the safety of the barn. But it was useless.

Finally, in frustration, the man said to himself, *If only I could become a bird for a few minutes. Then I could tell them the danger of the storm and how to get to safety.*

Suddenly the man realized what he'd just said. He finally understood what his wife and children had been telling him about Jesus. The only way God could tell us about the danger of sin and how to get to God and heaven was to become a man!

Now ask your kids these questions:

- **How does this story help you to better understand why Jesus had to come as a man?**
- **How are we like the sparrows?** (We wouldn't know about the dangers in life or the way to heaven without Jesus; we wouldn't know how to get to safety without someone telling us in words we can understand.)
- **What do you think it was like for Jesus to be like us?**
- **Jesus' message to us was that we must love God, love**

others, and believe that Jesus is God's Son. How are you doing in obeying Jesus' message?

- We know we can communicate with other humans. One message it's very important to communicate is about Jesus. Is there someone with whom you need to share God's message? Is there someone you need to tell about Jesus and what He did?

Take time to pray together for opportunities to share the message of God's love for us with those who haven't heard it.

WRAP-UP

Gather everyone in a circle and have family members take turns answering this question: **What's one thing you've learned about God today?**

Next, tell kids you've got a new "Life Slogan" you'd like to share with them.

Life Slogan: Today's Life Slogan is this: "Born on Christmas Day, God showed us the way!" Have family members repeat the slogan two or three times to help them learn it. Then encourage them to practice saying it during the week so they can talk about it at your next family night session.

Close in Prayer: Allow time for each family member to share prayer concerns and answers to prayer. Then close your time together with prayer for each concern. Thank God for listening to and caring about us.

Remember to record your prayer requests so you can refer to them in the future as you see God answering them.

Additional Resources:

The Night the Stars Danced for Joy by Bob Hartman (ages 4–8)
A Churchmouse Christmas by Barbara Davoll (ages 4–8)

8: Entrance Requirements

Exploring how a person gets into heaven

Scripture:
- Revelation 20:11-15 and 21:27—The importance of your name being in the book of life.
- Revelation 21:3-4, 10-27—Descriptions of heaven.

ACTIVITY OVERVIEW		
Activity	Summary	Pre-Session Prep
Activity 1: Knock, Knock	Enjoy jokes while thinking about places you can't get into by simply knocking.	You'll need a book of knock-knock jokes.
Activity 2: Let Me In!	Explore books of lists, determining how to get into various books.	You'll need a Bible, a phone book, a school yearbook, and other books as suggested in the activity.
Activity 3: Heaven Is a Wonderful Place	Discover what the Bible tells us we can expect in heaven.	You'll need a Bible and drawing supplies.

Main Points:

- —Some places aren't open to everyone.
- —Heaven is open to those whose names are in the book of life.
- —Heaven is where those whose names are in the book of life will spend eternity with God.

LIFE SLOGAN: "If your name is in the book, heaven's open—take a look!"

Make it your own
In the space provided below, outline the flow and add any additional ideas to guide you through the process of conducting this family night.

Prayer & Praise Items
In the space provided below, list any items you wish to pray about or give praise for during this family night session.

Journal
In the space provided below, capture a record of what fun or meaningful things which happened during this family night session.

Session Tip

We intentionally have provided more material than we would expect to be used in a single "Family Night" session. You know your family's unique interests and life circumstances best, so feel free to adapt this session to meet your family members' needs. Remember, short and simple is better than long and comprehensive.

WARM-UP

Open with Prayer: Begin by having a family member pray, asking God to help everyone in the family understand more about Him through this time. After prayer, review your last lesson by asking these questions:

- **What do you remember from our last lesson?**
- **How have you changed your actions in the last week because of what we learned last time?**
- **Do you remember the Life Slogan?**

Share: This week we're going to talk about getting into heaven.

ACTIVITY 1: Knock, Knock

Point: **Some places aren't open to everyone.**

Supplies: You'll need a book or magazine with "knock-knock" jokes in it. Check the children's section at your local library, or the bookshelves of your kids' rooms!

Activity: Start your family time with a few laughs. Read knock-knock jokes to your family. Use a book or magazine as a source of these corny jokes. Your kids probably know a few from school. Here are a few fun ones:

Knock, knock.
Who's there?
Sherwood.
Sherwood who?
Sherwood like to go out for ice cream right now!

Knock, knock.
Who's there?

Pastor.
Pastor who?
It's Pastor bedtime!

Knock, knock.
Who's there?
Alex.
Alex who?
Alex plain later.

When you've enjoyed laughing together, put away the joke books and discuss:

• **Where can you get in by simply knocking on the door?**
(Our house; a friend's house; Mom's office; etc.)

• **Have you ever knocked on someone's door and they wouldn't let you in? If so, what happened?**

• **What are places we want to get into that we might not be allowed?**

Answer might include an exclusive country club, a bank vault, a clique of popular students, an expensive school, or a sports team.

Share: Some places we can get into by just knocking on the door. Other places require membership—some kind of clearance, such as being a special agent with the government. Or it might mean knowing the right people. The most important place I want to get into is heaven. Let's talk about how to get into heaven.

ACTIVITY 2: Let Me In!

Point: Heaven is open to those whose names are in the book of life.

 Supplies: You'll need a Bible and a phone book and access to other books where names of family members may or may not be, such as the *Guinness Book of World Records*, a school yearbook, *Who's Who*, or other books of this nature. Find these at your local library.

Share: Let's find our names in as many books as possible.

Age Adjustments

VERY YOUNG CHILDREN may not understand the puns in knock-knock jokes, but they'll enjoy laughing with the rest of the family. Even if they make up jokes with nonsense punch lines, be sure to laugh along. However, young children will certainly understand knocking at doors. Being too small to reach doorknobs means they're *always* knocking!

Read the story of the *Three Little Pigs* to young children. They'll laugh along as the Big Bad Wolf tries to get into the homes of the pigs, and will understand why the pigs won't let him in.

Activity: Look through the phone book, school yearbook, and other books where you know your names will be listed. Also look in books such as the *Guinness Book of World Records, Who's Who in America,* rosters for professional sports teams, and so on. (If you or any of your family members are listed in these books, congratulations!)

Discuss these questions:

- **Why are our names in some books and not in others?** (Some books are general listings; some books require membership or other qualifications. For example, Dad isn't listed in the school yearbook because he's not a student there. Jimmy isn't listed in the phone book because he doesn't pay the phone bill.)

- **What kinds of books do people try to get their names into?** (Authors try to get their names on books by publishing; athletes try to get their names in record books; scientists try to get their names in professional journals; movie stars want people to write books about them.)

- **Why do you think people want their names in books?** (So others will think they're important; so they can get recognition for what they've done; so others will remember them and what they've accomplished.)

> ## Age Adjustments
>
> Hell can be a frightening concept for CHILDREN OF ALL AGES. Use your own judgment regarding how much you want to explain to your children regarding the realities of hell. However, don't sugarcoat the sadness and pain of hell so your children won't be frightened. Hell is a terrible, awful place, and we don't want to go there!
>
> OLDER CHILDREN can look up further references where the Bible mentions the book of life. These verses tell about those who are in the book of life and what happens to those who aren't listed in this book. Try Psalm 69:28, Philippians 4:3, and Revelation 13:8 and 17:8. What do you learn from these verses about the importance of the book of life?

Share: The most important book to have our name in is in heaven. It's the book of life. Let's see what the Bible says about this book.

 Read Revelation 20:11-15 and 21:27 aloud, then ask the following questions:

- **Do you think anyone can get into heaven?** (Yes, but *only* if their name is in the book of life.)

- **What's required to get into heaven?** (Reference John 3:16— If we believe in Jesus' death and resurrection, our names will be in the book of life. That's the requirement.)

- **What happens if your name isn't found in the book of life?** (You will be thrown into a lake of fire, or hell.)

Share: We might not be smart enough or athletic enough or powerful enough to have our names in a lot of special books. But anyone, no matter how smart, athletic, or powerful, can have their name in the book of life. It's as easy as believing in Jesus as your Lord! And if your name is in the book of life, you won't be left knocking at heaven's gate. God will be welcoming you inside!

Note: If you're unsure as to whether or not your children understand how to become a Christian, refer to "How to Lead Your Child to Christ" on pages 115–117 of this book.

ACTIVITY 3: Heaven Is a Wonderful Place

Point: Heaven is where those whose names are in the book of life will spend eternity with God.

Supplies: You'll need a Bible and drawing supplies, such as paper, pencils, markers, or crayons.

Activity: Give each family member blank pieces of paper and drawing materials, such as markers or crayons. Ask everyone to draw a picture of what they think heaven looks like.

After each person has completed their pictures, take turns going around and letting each one tell about his or her picture of heaven. Even if a child thinks heaven is like Disneyland, don't ridicule! This is a time of sharing, so allow everyone to express their thoughts.

Share: People use their imaginations to help them think of what heaven will be like. Some think we'll be floating around on clouds, while others think there will be nothing to do but play golf all day! We don't know everything about heaven, but we can read what the Bible tells us about it.

Read Revelation 21:3-4, 10-27 aloud and discuss:

- **What does the Bible say heaven will be like?** (There will be no death, no mourning or crying; it's like a square city; the walls and streets are made of gold, jasper, sapphire, emeralds, and other precious stones; God is there and we will live with Him; there will be no sin there.)

• What part of heaven sounds best to you?

Share: We don't know everything about heaven, and it's fun to imagine all the wonderful things God has created there for us. It will be exciting to be with other followers of God from the beginning of time. But the best part of heaven is that we'll get to be with God! That's why it's important to have your name written in the book of life. We want to spend eternity with God!

WRAP-UP

Gather everyone in a circle and have family members take turns answering this question: **What's one thing you've learned about God today?**

Next, tell kids you've got a new "Life Slogan" you'd like to share with them.

> ## Age Adjustments
>
> YOUNGER CHILDREN may not be as excited about heaven, as it seems to be an abstract place associated with death. They may be reassured by thinking of loved ones they'll get to see in heaven, such as grandparents who have passed away. Basically, young children want to know someone will love them and take care of them.

Life Slogan: Today's Life Slogan is this: **"If your name is in the book, heaven's open—take a look!"** Have family members repeat the slogan two or three times to help them learn it. Then encourage them to practice saying it during the week so they can talk about it at your next family night session.

Close in Prayer: Allow time for each family member to share prayer concerns and answers to prayer. Then close your time together with prayer for each concern. Thank God for listening to and caring about us.

Remember to record your prayer requests so you can refer to them in the future as you see God answering them.

Additional Resources:

Let's Talk About Heaven by Debby Anderson (ages 4–8)

© 9: Born Twice?

Exploring what it means to be born again

Scripture
• John 3—Nicodemus asks Jesus about being born again.
• 2 Corinthians 5:17—We have a new life in Christ.

ACTIVITY OVERVIEW		
Activity	Summary	Pre-Session Prep
Activity 1: Nic at Night	Learn the story of Nicodemus and Jesus.	You'll need a Bible, paper and pencil, and costumes (if desired).
Activity 2: Changed Forever	Learn about how "all things become new."	You'll need a video or picture book showing a caterpillar changing into a butterfly.

Main Points:
   —We must be born again to have eternal life
   —When we are born again, we are changed forever!

LIFE SLOGAN: "Born once, same old you. Born twice, all things new."

Make it your own

In the space provided below, outline the flow and add any additional ideas to guide you through the process of conducting this family night.

Prayer & Praise Items

In the space provided below, list any items you wish to pray about or give praise for during this family night session.

Journal

In the space provided below, capture a record of what fun or meaningful things which happened during this family night session.

Session Tip

We intentionally have provided more material than we would expect to be used in a single "Family Night" session. You know your family's unique interests and life circumstances best, so feel free to adapt this session to meet your family members' needs. Remember, short and simple is better than long and comprehensive.

 ## WARM-UP

Open with Prayer: Begin by having a family member pray, asking God to help everyone in the family understand more about Him through this time. After prayer, review your last lesson by asking these questions:

- **What did we learn about in our last lesson?**
- **What was something fun we did in our last lesson?**
- **Do you remember the Life Slogan?**

Share: Perhaps you've heard people say that Christians are "born again." Today we'll discover where that term came from and what it means.

ACTIVITY 1: Nic at Night

Point: We must be born again to have eternal life.

Supplies: You'll need a Bible, paper and pencil, and costumes, if desired.

Activity: Tell your family that it's show time! You'll be working together to put on a short play from the Bible.

Ask each child to "try out" for a part—you'll be assigning the parts of Nicodemus and Jesus to two of the children. (Note: Allow each child the opportunity to try each part, if they wish.) Explain that before acting, actors must understand the characters they will be playing in order to properly do the part.

Give the child playing the part of Nicodemus a piece of paper with the following questions listed. Help them develop the answers as a "character study" before trying out for the part.

• **What do you think Nicodemus looked like?** (Let the child be as creative as they like on this one.)

• **Nicodemus was a Pharisee. What were Pharisees like?** (Ask each child to share anything they might know about the Pharisees. Drawing from their knowledge and/or the "About Pharisees" section below, list some of the characteristics of Nicodemus that will help the child act the part.)

• **What kind of clothes did he probably wear?** (The clothes of a wealthy, religious leader. You may want to help the child find a "costume" to look the part.)

• **Why do you think Nicodemus come to Jesus at night rather than during the day?** (He was probably embarrassed to let other people see him asking Jesus questions because Pharisees were supposed to "know it all.")

Follow the same process for the character of Jesus, asking the following questions.

• **What kind of person was Jesus?** (Kind, loving, strong, etc.)

• **With whom did Jesus spend most of His time?** (The common people, sinners, the poor, etc.)

• **What kind of clothes would Jesus have been wearing?** (The clothes of a carpenter—not fancy. Again, find an appropriate costume.)

• **Would Jesus have been impressed by or intimidated by the Pharisees?** (No. In fact, He often confronted them.)

About Pharisees

PHARISEES WERE . . .

• **Leaders**—religious teachers in the time of Jesus
• **Strict**—demanding that the people obey their harsh and man-made rules
• **Proud**—thought of themselves as much better than the common people
• **Angry**—mad at Jesus because He was teaching God's love rather than their rules
• **Powerful**—many Pharisees were part of the Jewish ruling council

Share: Now that you've completed your character study it is time to read the story in order to develop the script.

Read John 3 and pull out key lines and write them on a separate page to be used as each child's script. There should be three parts—Nicodemus, Jesus, and a narrator to read all nonacted sections.

Once the script has been completed, get into the costumes and act out the play. Keep in mind that you want the children to try to feel and think like Nicodemus and Jesus.

Note: Have fun "directing" them as if you are a professional movie director. Use lines such as "Action!" and "Cut!" and "Role

Tape!" to create the right environment. You may even want to create a makeshift megaphone to shout orders.

Also, if you are acting one of the parts, you may want to insert a few out-of-character lines to cause a reaction from the others. For example, you may replace Jesus' "you must be born again" line with "you must obey all my rules"—which provides the opportunity to highlight the difference between Jesus' teaching and that of the Pharisees.

After acting the play, ask the children the following questions:
- **Why was the term "born again" so confusing to Nicodemus?** (He thought it meant physical birth.)
- **What did Jesus mean by "born again"?** (Spiritual birth.)
- **According to John 3:16, what does a person have to do to be born again?** (Believe in Jesus as God's Son.)
- **What happens when we are born again?** (We "won't perish" and we will receive "eternal life.")

Share: Nicodemus came to Jesus because he was curious about what Jesus had to say. He came with an open mind and an open heart. He came without someone forcing him to come. That's the way we must come to Jesus too. Each of us must make a decision to believe in Jesus on our own. I can't make that decision for you, and you can't make it for me.

Age Adjustments

FOR YOUNGER CHILDREN, read this story account from a Bible storybook, or paraphrase the story at a level they can understand.

Note: The kids may be glad to learn that Nicodemus took Jesus' words seriously. The Bible mentions him two other times. The first, in John 7:50-51, tells of Nicodemus defending Jesus against other Pharisees. The second, in John 19:39-40, explains how he helped prepare Jesus' body for burial.

ACTIVITY 2: Changed Forever

Point: When we are born again, we are changed forever.

 Supplies: You'll need a video or picture book showing a caterpillar forming a cocoon and emerging as a butterfly (check your local library). A tadpole becoming a frog or a seed growing into a plant would also work. Adjust questions to the object you are using.

Activity: Show the video or pictures, then discuss:
- **How was the caterpillar "born again"?** (It was changed into something completely new.)
- **How is this like or unlike being spiritually born again?** (We are changed inside vs. outside; we become something different than we were; we live on a new level; etc.)
- **What is different for the caterpillar now that it is a butterfly?** (It is beautiful rather than ugly; it can fly vs. crawl; etc.)
- **What is different for us after we are born again?** (We are forgiven for our sins; we have eternal life with God; we have a relationship with God; etc.)

Reread John 3:3, then ask...
- **Is there any way for the caterpillar to become a butterfly other than going through its "rebirth"?** (No.)
- **Is there any way we can have eternal life without being born again?** (No. See John 3:3)
- **Can the butterfly go back to being a caterpillar?** (No.)

Share: Just as caterpillars are permanently changed when they become butterflies, so we are permanently changed when we become born again.

 Read 2 Corinthians 5:17 together, then ask . . .
- **What becomes new when we are born again?** (Everything!)
- **What became new for the caterpillar when it was reborn?** (Everything!)
- **Do you think it would be better to live as a caterpillar or a butterfly? Why?**
- **Do you think it is better to "perish" or have "eternal life"?**

Share: Being born again changes us forever—and there is no going back to a caterpillar life!

Note: If your child has not yet taken the step of believing in Jesus, and if this lesson has sparked a desire to do so in him or her, you may want to go to the appendix on page 115 entitled "How to Lead Your Child to Christ" and take advantage of the opportunity to do so.

WRAP-UP
Gather everyone in a circle and have family members take turns answering this question: **What's one thing you've learned about God today?**

Next, tell kids you've got a new "Life Slogan" you'd like to share with them.

Life Slogan: Today's Life Slogan is this: "Born once, same old you. Born twice, all things new." Have family members repeat the slogan two or three times to help them learn it. Then encourage them to practice saying it during the week so they can talk about it at your next family night session.

Close in Prayer: Allow time for each family member to share prayer concerns and answers to prayer. Then close your time together with prayer for each concern. Thank God for listening to and caring about us.

Remember to record your prayer requests so you can refer to them in the future as you see God answering them.

Additional Resources:

The Toddlers Bible by V. Gilbert Beers (ages 1–3)
You Too Can Know Jesus (ages 4–7)

@ 10: Turn Around!

Exploring what it means to repent from our sin

Scripture
- Romans 3:23—Everyone misses God's target.
- 2 Samuel 11:1–12:14 —The story of David and Bathsheba.
- Luke 3:8 and Acts 26:20—Our actions show our repentance.
- Galatians 5:22-23—The fruit of the Spirit.

ACTIVITY OVERVIEW		
Activity	Summary	Pre-Session Prep
Activity 1: Eggs-cuse Me!	See the mess that's made by missing the target.	You'll need raw eggs, a small bucket of water, and a Bible.
Activity 2: One Thing Leads to Another	Look at the mess of sin made by David.	You'll need a Bible.
Activity 3: Turn Around	Play a game to learn the meaning of repentance.	You'll need a blindfold and a Bible.

Main Points:

—All of us make a mess by sinning.

—No matter how big of a mess we make with our sins, God still loves us.

—We repent by turning away from sin and toward God.

LIFE SLOGAN: "When we sin, we disobey. So repent and go the other way."

Make it your own

In the space provided below, outline the flow and add any additional ideas to guide you through the process of conducting this family night.

Prayer & Praise Items

In the space provided below, list any items you wish to pray about or give praise for during this family night session.

Journal

In the space provided below, capture a record of what fun or meaningful things which happened during this family night session.

Session Tip

We intentionally have provided more material than we would expect to be used in a single "Family Night" session. You know your family's unique interests and life circumstances best, so feel free to adapt this session to meet your family members' needs. Remember, short and simple is better than long and comprehensive.

 WARM-UP

Open with Prayer: Begin by having a family member pray, asking God to help everyone in the family understand more about Him through this time. After prayer, review your last lesson by asking these questions:

• **What do you remember from our last lesson?**
• **Do you remember the Life Slogan?**

Share: Sometimes we go in the wrong direction in life. Today we're going to learn how to turn around!

ACTIVITY 1: Eggs-cuse Me!

Point: All of us make a mess by sinning.

 **Supplies:** You'll need raw eggs, a small bucket of water, and a Bible.

Activity: Take your family outside to your driveway or a sidewalk area. (You might want to choose an area near your hose!) Indicate an imaginary line on the ground and have everyone stand with their toes along this line. Give each person one egg.

Set the bucket of water about five feet from where family members are standing. Then explain that each person should toss his or her egg into the bucket without breaking it. Be sure to mention that anyone who breaks an egg must clean up the mess.

Begin the tossing. If anyone makes it into the bucket without breaking his or her egg, have that person retrieve the egg, move back another foot, and toss again. Continue until

Instead of Eggs

If you can't afford to use this many eggs, or are simply uncomfortable using food in this manner, substitute water balloons. It doesn't have quite the same messy effect, but will work just as well.

89

each person has broken his or her egg. Then pull out the hose and have everyone help in cleaning up the mess.

Then gather together and discuss:
- **Was it easy or hard for you to hit the target? Explain your answer.**
- **What happened when you missed the target?** (The egg broke; it made a big mess!)
- **Is there any way for you to put the egg and its contents back together again? Why not?**
- **Let's compare our game to real life. How do we miss the target with God?** (Answers might include not doing what we know is right; disobeying parents, teachers, or employers; or any other sin.)
- **How do we make a mess of things when we sin?** (We get in trouble; we get punished; we hurt other people; we hurt feelings; and so on.)
- **How is this like breaking an egg?** (We can't change the actions we've done, just like we can't put an egg back together.)
- **Is there anyone who doesn't sin?**

Read Romans 3:23 as an answer to this. *All* have sinned.

Share: Sin is missing the target by not doing what God wants us to do. When we miss the target, we can make a big mess out of things. I wonder if this changes how God feels about us. Let's find out!

ACTIVITY 2: One Thing Leads to Another

Point: No matter how big of a mess we make with our sins, God still loves us.

 Supplies: You'll need a Bible.

Share: When we sin, sometimes we hurt others and sometimes we hurt ourselves. When we lie, we face the consequences of being found out. When we disobey, we face being punished. When people have sex before marriage, they might get a disease or become parents before they're ready. Those who take drugs can permanently damage their bodies or even go to jail. If I steal from my work, I would lose my job.

See if family members can remember any recent times when they've sinned, and what the consequences of that sin were. Then discuss this question:

- **When does God love you more—when you obey Him or when you have messed up?**

After discussion, share: **The answer might surprise you! God loves you just the same either way, because His love is unconditional. Do you know what that means? It means that God loves you no matter what you do. He doesn't love us because we obey Him. Instead, we obey Him because we love Him! So when we mess up and sin, we can ask God to forgive us.**

God always forgives us, but sometimes we still have to live with the consequences of what we did wrong. For example, if you steal candy from a store, I would still love you, but you would still have to be punished. It's the same with God. In fact, a story in the Bible helps us understand more about how God forgives us when we sin, but we still have to live with the consequences of what we've done.

 Read 2 Samuel 11:1–12:14 aloud to your family, then discuss:

- **What did David do wrong?** (He slept with a woman who was not his wife. In fact, she was the wife of another man.)
- **What were the consequences of this?** (She became pregnant.)
- **How did David try to clean up his mess?** (He caused Bathsheba's husband to be killed, thus making an even bigger mess.)
- **What were the consequences of this?** (David and Bathsheba's baby died.)
- **Does this story tell you that God stopped loving David?** (No. God still loved David, but David was still punished.)

Share: **By sinning, David missed God's target and made a big mess of his life and the lives of others. But David asked God to forgive him for his terrible sins, and God did. David was punished, but God still loved David and continued to use David for His good.**

Age Adjustments

FOR YOUNGER CHILDREN, read the story of David and Bathsheba from a children's Bible story book, or retell the story in words they'll understand. Also for younger children, the point of one sin leading to another and causing a bigger and bigger mess is humorously and pointedly explored in the Veggie Tales video "Larry-Boy and the Fib from Outer Space." Your entire family (even teenagers!) is sure to enjoy this show.

FOR OLDER CHILDREN, read Psalm 51 and discuss how David felt about his sins after being confronted by Nathan. How do we respond when we're confronted with our sins? How should we respond?

OLDER CHILDREN might also be able to think of times when they've tried to cover up for a wrongdoing, only to make the situation bigger and bigger.

ACTIVITY 3: Turn Around

Point: We repent by turning away from sin and toward God.

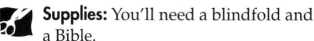 **Supplies:** You'll need a blindfold and a Bible.

Activity: Ask one child to be a volunteer. Blindfold this child, then explain you'll give this child a simple task to complete while blindfolded. For example, you might have the child go into her room, touch her pillow, then return to the living room.

Share: Any time you're about to walk into something, the rest of us will yell out, "Repent!" This will be your clue to turn around.

Begin the activity, with family members following the child on her task and calling out, "Repent!" before she stubs her toes or walks into doors.

Then return to the living room and choose another family member to be blindfolded. Repeat the activity until all family members have had a chance to participate, but be sure to save yourself for last.

When it's finally your turn to be blindfolded, begin as the others did. But when you're warned with "Repent!" answer loudly, "I don't need to repent!" and continue on your way, banging into furniture and crashing your knees. Be sure to go gently on yourself, but your kids will get a kick out of your hamming it up with your injuries.

When you've finally finished bumbling your way through your task, gather everyone together to discuss the following question:

- **Does this game give you any idea as to what it means to repent?**

After giving family members time to tell what they think, share: To repent means to turn around and go the other way.

- **Why was it important to repent in our game?** (You might walk into a wall; you won't be able to finish the task.)
- **How is repenting different from saying you're sorry?**

Share: When you say you're sorry, you're showing sadness or remorse for your actions. When you repent, you stop doing what is

wrong and do what is right. It's sort of like showing you're sorry by your actions.

- **Why does God want us to repent?** (God wants us to go His way.)
- **What happens when we don't repent?** (We keep getting hurt or hurting others; we aren't going God's way; we still get punished.)

Share: When I refused to repent in our game, I crashed into things and caused damage. In real life when we don't repent, we can get into even more trouble! We'll keep making a mess of things. Let's see what the Bible says about all this.

Age Adjustments

FOR OLDER CHILDREN AND TEENS, discuss these questions: How does the saying "Actions speak louder than words" compare to the principle of repentance? How does your life demonstrate this?

 Read Luke 3:8 and Acts 26:20 together, then ask:
- **What might be some "fruits of repentance" our lives could show?** (Showing we're not selfish by giving to others; showing we're not cheaters by our actions; instead of spreading gossip about others, using your words to encourage others and share love.)
- **How do we prove that we've repented?** (By our actions.)

Read Galatians 5:22-23, then **share: These verses tell us what God expects us to do when we've sinned. God wants us to ask for forgiveness and be sorry, but it's very important that we repent, or turn around and do what's right instead of what's wrong.**

WRAP-UP

Gather everyone in a circle and have family members take turns answering this question: **What's one thing you've learned about God today?**

Next, tell kids you've got a new "Life Slogan" you'd like to share with them.

Life Slogan: Today's Life Slogan is this: "When we sin, we disobey. So repent and go the other way!" Have family members repeat the slogan two or three times to help them learn it. Then encourage them to practice saying it during the week so they can talk about it at your next family night session.

Close in Prayer: Allow time for each family member to share prayer concerns and answers to prayer. Then close your time together with prayer for each concern. Thank God for listening to and caring about us.

Remember to record your prayer requests so you can refer to them in the future as you see God answering them.

Additional Resources:

Caution: Dangerous Devotions by Jackie Persghetti (ages 8–12)

@ 11: A Walk in the PARK

Exploring how the Holy Spirit helps us

Scripture:
• John 14:15-17—Jesus promises to send the Holy Spirit.
• Acts 2:1-4—The Holy Spirit comes.
• Acts 1:8 and Ephesians 3:16-17—The Holy Spirit gives us power.
• Romans 8:26-27—The Holy Spirit helps us pray.
• 1 Corinthians 2:11-16—The Holy Spirit helps us know what God wants us to do.
• Ephesians 1:17—The Holy Spirit gives us knowledge.

ACTIVITY OVERVIEW

Activity	Summary	Pre-Session Prep
Activity 1: Shape Up!	Guide each other in a drawing exercise.	You'll need the "picture" on page 103, paper, pencils, and erasers.
Activity 2: The PARK Guide	Explore what the Bible says about the Holy Spirit.	You'll need a Bible.
Activity 3: Helping Hands	Undertake a chore with a lot of help.	Supplies will vary depending on the task you choose.

Main Points:

—We need help in life.
—The Holy Spirit helps us in many ways.
—With help, life is a lot easier!

LIFE SLOGAN: Walking in the Spirit is like a walk in the PARK. Walking without the Spirit is like walking in the dark!

Make it your own

In the space provided below, outline the flow and add any additional ideas to guide you through the process of conducting this family night.

Prayer & Praise Items

In the space provided below, list any items you wish to pray about or give praise for during this family night session.

Journal

In the space provided below, capture a record of what fun or meaningful things which happened during this family night session.

Session Tip

We intentionally have provided more material than we would expect to be used in a single "Family Night" session. You know your family's unique interests and life circumstances best, so feel free to adapt this session to meet your family members' needs. Remember, short and simple is better than long and comprehensive.

WARM-UP

Open with Prayer: Begin by having a family member pray, asking God to help everyone in the family understand more about Him through this time. After prayer, review your last lesson by asking these questions:

• **What do you remember from our last lesson?**
• **Do you remember the Life Slogan?**
• **How have your actions changed because of what we learned?** Encourage family members to give specific examples of how they've applied what was learned in recent lessons.

Share: Sometimes people think it would be easier to be a Christian if Jesus were still living as a human among us. But Jesus didn't leave us alone when He went back to His Father. He sent a Helper. Today we're going to learn about that Helper.

ACTIVITY 1: Shape Up!

Point: We need help in life.

Supplies: You'll need the geometric drawing on page 103, a sheet of blank paper for each family member, and pencils with erasers.

Activity: Give each family member a blank sheet of paper and a pencil with an eraser. For your own use, look at the geometric drawing on page 103, but don't let anyone else in the family see this picture.

Explain: **I have a picture here that uses four different shapes. I'm going to explain to you how to draw the picture. You can ask**

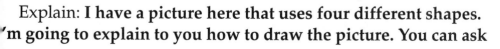

questions, and I'll try to guide you into drawing what I have in mind.

Without showing family members the picture, do your best to give directions as to how they should be replicating the picture. For example, "Begin by drawing a large square near the top of your page. Now you'll be drawing a triangle . . ." As family members get various parts correct, compliment them on how they're doing. If family members are having trouble putting down your instructions, gently make suggestions as to how their drawing could be changed. Don't do the drawing for them, and don't criticize if they misunderstand your directions. You're the only guide they have on this, so if they're doing it wrong, it's largely your problem!

When everyone's artwork is as close to perfection as you think it ever will be, show the picture and let everyone compare how well they did. If family members enjoyed this, let one of the children draw another geometric design and try to instruct family members (including you) on how to replicate it. The activity can be repeated again so everyone gets a chance to be the leader.

Age Adjustments

YOUNGER CHILDREN may not be able to do the drawing exercise, or it may be too abstract for them. Instead, play a game where you tell your children three simple tasks, then they must remember them and do them in the correct order. For example, turn in a circle, do two jumping jacks, then hide in the closet. Let them also have a turn giving you tasks to remember. After the game is over, discuss what tasks would be too hard for them to do (light a fire, move furniture). Then remind them that you'll never ask them to do more than they can handle, and God doesn't either.

When all drawings are completed, put away your artwork and discuss these questions:

- **Which did you think was harder, being the one giving directions or being the one following directions? Explain.**
- **What would have made this activity easier for you?**
- **This was just for fun, but sometimes we do have to follow the directions of others. Sometimes this is easy and sometimes it's hard. Can you think of a time it was easy to follow the directions of another person?**

Possible answers might include making a bed, writing your name on your paper, or other very simple tasks.

- **When is it difficult to follow someone else's directions?**
  Possible answers might include these: when the directions are long or complicated; when you don't understand the directions; when you don't understand much about the task; when the task itself is too hard to do.
- **What directions has God given us that seem hard to you?**

Answers will vary depending on the personal struggles of each family member. In this discussion you might want to question what it is that God actually directs us to do. This might include directions such as the Ten Commandments, or you might simply summarize all the commandments by reading Luke 10:27.

Share: Sometimes it seems hard to know exactly what God wants us to do. Other people have felt the same way.

ACTIVITY 2: The PARK Guide

Point: The Holy Spirit helps us in many ways.

 Supplies: You'll need a Bible.

Share: The people who were probably most unsure about following God's directions were Jesus' followers when they found out Jesus wouldn't be here on earth with them forever.

Before Jesus died on the cross and rose again, He was having dinner with His friends and told them He'd be going away soon. They became nervous and afraid about this. What were they supposed to do? Who would they follow? They had a lot of questions. Let's read what Jesus told them.

 Read John 14:15-17 aloud, then pose these questions:
- **Who is the "Counselor," or "Spirit of truth," Jesus mentions here?** (The Holy Spirit.)
- **Why do you think Jesus calls the Holy Spirit by these names?** (The Holy Spirit gives us advice like a counselor would; the Holy Spirit always leads us toward truth; the Holy Spirit is truth.)

Share: It wasn't long after this dinner that Jesus was arrested, hung on the cross to die, and then rose again. After some time with His followers, Jesus returned to heaven.

(If you like, you can read about this in Acts 1:1-11.)

Share: Jesus' followers were afraid after this. They didn't know what to do without their leader. But what Jesus promised came true.

 Read Acts 2:1-4 together.

Share: We don't see the Holy Spirit like fire anymore, and don't hear

the Holy Spirit as wind. But this was how the Holy Spirit came the first time, giving strength, courage, and leading to the disciples so they'd do what Jesus had commanded them to do.

Just like Jesus was also God, so the Holy Spirit is also God.

This can be difficult to explain, especially to young children. Here is a simple breakdown of the roles of the Trinity:

- God the Father is completely in control. He's the *planner* of all things. He's the only one who knows when the end of our world will be.
- God the Son is the *performer* of the plan. He came to earth to do what God wanted Him to do.
- God the Holy Spirit is the *provider of power* to us so we can carry on God's work.

Share: I know a simple way for us to understand how the Spirit helps us and gives us power to do what God wants.

Take a large sheet of paper and use a marker to write PARK down the left side of the paper.

Share: When we live without God, without the Holy Spirit, it's like we're walking in the dark. There's no one to lead us or help us know what's true. But when we let the Holy Spirit guide us, it's like a walk in the park! Here's how.

Beside each letter write the following sentences, then discuss their meanings with the questions that follow:

P—POWER TO OBEY GOD

 Read Acts 1:8 and Ephesians 3:16-17.

- **What kind of power do these verses say the Spirit gives us?** (Power to tell others about Jesus; power to let Christ rule our attitudes and actions.)

A—ASSISTS US IN PRAYER

 Read Romans 8:26-27.

- **How does the Holy Spirit assist us in prayer?** (Helps us know what to pray for; expresses things we cannot express; prays as a representative for us.)

Read 1 Corinthians 2:11-16.

• **How does the Holy Spirit let us know what God wants for us?** (By helping us understand spiritual matters; by helping us understand what God has given us; by helping us think as Christ would think.)

Share: On this point, think back to the drawing activity. One family member gave directions to help others know what to do. How is this like the Holy Spirit revealing or guiding us toward what God wants us to do?

K—KNOWLEDGE

Read Ephesians 1:17.

• **What kind of knowledge does the Holy Spirit give us? (**Wisdom; knowledge to know more about Jesus; knowledge of what is right and what is wrong)

Share: These are just a few of the things the Bible teaches us about the Holy Spirit.

ACTIVITY 3: Helping Hands

Point: With help, life is a lot easier!

 Supplies: You'll need supplies to do the chore you choose.

Activity: Choose any chore that your family can do together. This might be raking the yard; washing, drying, and putting away dishes; cleaning out the garage; or weeding the garden.

With a spirit of joyful enthusiasm, lead your family in undertaking this task. Put on some cheerful music, or sing together as you work. Or tell knock-knock jokes, making up as many new ones as you can.

Age Adjustments

This discussion is too long for VERY YOUNG CHILDREN. Focus only on the PARK section, briefly sharing how the Holy Spirit helps us.

Another way to help younger children understand more about the Trinity is an explanation like this that can be adjusted to your own family situation:

You are a daughter, a sister, a student, and a friend. Or an adult might be a dad, husband, friend, employee, and a neighbor. One person has more than one identity. God has three identities as the Father, Son, and Holy Spirit. This is a simplistic look at the Trinity, but it sometimes helps children understand how God can be three beings.

OLDER CHILDREN AND TEENAGERS may want to discuss the topic of speaking in tongues that is brought up in Acts 2. If you're unsure about what you or your denomination believe on this topic, talk with your pastor or check your local Christian bookstore for books on the topic.

During the time of working together, discuss how much easier it is to get a job done when the whole family joyfully pitches in. Compare this to how the Holy Spirit gladly helps us in living as God wants us to live. You could take the comparison further and discuss how much more of God's work would be completed if all Christians had a cheerful attitude of helping.

After the work is done, thank everyone for helping. You might want to complete your time together by taking a walk in the park!

WRAP-UP

Gather everyone in a circle and have family members take turns answering this question: **What's one thing you've learned about God today?**

Next, tell kids you've got a new "Life Slogan" you'd like to share with them.

Life Slogan: Today's Life Slogan is this: "Walking in the Spirit is like a walk in the PARK. Walking without the Spirit is like walking in the dark!"

Have family members repeat the slogan two or three times to help them learn it. Then encourage them to practice saying it during the week so they can talk about it at your next family night session.

Close in Prayer: Allow time for each family member to share prayer concerns and answers to prayer. Then close your time together with prayer for each concern. Thank God for listening to and caring about us.

Remember to record your prayer requests so you can refer to them in the future as you see God answering them.

Additional Resources:

Discovery Bible Devotions (ages 8–12)
Psalms for a Child's Heart by Sheryl Crawford (ages 4–8)

GEOMETRIC DRAWING

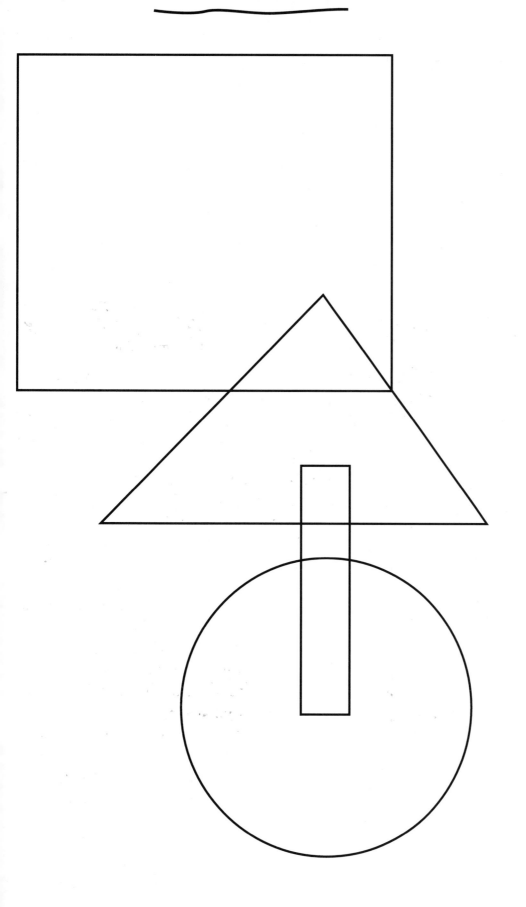

⊚ 12: Family Ties

Exploring God's purposes for families

Scripture:
• Ephesians 5:22-33—The responsibilities of husbands and wives.
• Ephesians 6:1-4—The responsibilities of parents and children.
• Proverbs 27:17—We can "sharpen" each other.

ACTIVITY OVERVIEW		
Activity	Summary	Pre-Session Prep
Activity 1: Memory Lane	Discover how your family was created and God's plan for your family.	You'll need family photo albums and a Bible.
Activity 2: Special Blend	Affirm the special gift each person brings to make your family unlike any other.	You'll need paint, tooth-picks, white paper, and a Bible.
Activity 3: Stiff Support	Learn how family members can help each other even when they can't help them-selves.	You'll need masking tape, a bowl of unwrapped can-dies, a Bible, and sticks as described in the lesson.

Main Points:

—God made us a special family.

—God made our family unique by placing each of us in it.

—God made families to help each other.

LIFE SLOGAN: "God so loved me, He made my family!"

Make it your own

In the space provided below, outline the flow and add any additional ideas to guide you through the process of conducting this family night.

Prayer & Praise Items

In the space provided below, list any items you wish to pray about or give praise for during this family night session.

Journal

In the space provided below, capture a record of what fun or meaningful things which happened during this family night session.

Session Tip

We intentionally have provided more material than we would expect to be used in a single "Family Night" session. You know your family's unique interests and life circumstances best, so feel free to adapt this session to meet your family members' needs. Remember, short and simple is better than long and comprehensive.

WARM-UP

Open with Prayer: Begin by having a family member pray, asking God to help everyone in the family understand more about Him through this time. After prayer, review your last lesson by asking these questions:

- **What do you remember from our last lesson?**
- **Do you remember the Life Slogan?**
- **What was one fun thing we did during our last lesson?**
- **How has what we learned last week changed your actions in the past few days?**

Share: Today we're going to learn about why families are so important. The best way to get started is to talk about our family!

ACTIVITY 1: Memory Lane

Point: God made us a special family.

Supplies: You'll need family photo albums and a Bible.

Activity: Bring out your family photo albums and huddle together so everyone can see them. Begin by looking at pictures of both parents before they were married. Each parent may want to recall and share a little about what their lives were like before they married, or what their family was like when they were growing up.

Then move to your wedding pictures, talking about how you met, courted, were engaged, and finally married. Tell special memories of your wedding day—perhaps a funny story or tender moment you shared. Explain how now your lives are blended by the vows you took and by your love for each other.

Move on through the albums, to the point of each child's birth. Share about the excitement surrounding each new life joining your family. Talk about how each child changed the family, adding to it and creating something new.

After you've looked at the pictures, ask:

- **What makes our family different from other families?**
- **What's something special you like about our family?**
- **Why do you think God made families?**

There are many possible answers to this last question. Some answers your family might suggest are:

- So we can grow and be cared for by people who love us.
- To give us a place to learn how to work together and honor, respect, and serve others.
- To let us have security, forgiveness, and guidelines for living.
- To help us learn about God's love from the love of our family members.

Share: Let's look in the Bible to see what we can find out about families.

Families Are Different

Your family may not be a traditional family. Perhaps you're a grandparent, single parent, or part of a blended family. When viewing pictures together, adapt the discussion as is appropriate for your family situation. Make this a positive time, focusing on what makes your family special. If your situation involves a family separation, avoid focusing on the faults of the separated individual or individuals. Instead, remember the good things about family members. Strongly remind your children that although families are different, your family is special.

 Read Ephesians 5:22-24 and discuss these questions:
- **How would you say this in your own words?**
- **What do you think it means?**

Share: This verse tells us that just like the church submits to Christ, so wives submit to their husbands. Wives show their submission by respecting and following their husbands.

 Read Ephesians 5:25-33 and discuss:
- **What do these verses seem to be saying?**
- **How does the husband submit himself?** (A husband submits himself by loving and serving his wife.)

Share: These verses remind us that Jesus loved us so much that He died for us. In the same way, husbands should love and respect their

wives so much that they'd be willing to die for them. Husbands should show more love for their wives than for themselves.

Take a risk by asking your children to rate how you and your spouse are doing in this area. Don't be defensive if they point out areas for growth. Take it as an honest word of advice on how to better show love for your spouse.

Share: Now let's find out about the role of children.

 Read Ephesians 6:1-4 and ask:
- **What's the most important thing God wants children to do?** (The most important thing is obey.)
- **Why do you think obeying is so important to God?**

Share: God wants children to obey for several reasons. One is that we learn to obey God by obeying our parents. Another is that we are often protected from danger by obeying our parents.
- **What special advice is given to parents?**
- **What does this mean?**

Share: God doesn't want parents to make life too hard for their kids. Parents should challenge their children and teach them about God. That's one reason we have these family times! But parents shouldn't make unreasonable demands on their children or discourage them too much.

Again, if you're willing to take the risk, ask your children if they think you're too hard on them. This may give you an opportunity to briefly explain why you ask them to do certain things, or why you've set specific rules. However, be sure to listen to their concerns with an open mind. You may discover something—such as sarcasm, anger, or another area—where you're harming your children and making life unpleasant for them. Take these comments in with careful consideration as areas for growth in parenting.

Age Adjustments

YOUNGER CHILDREN will enjoy looking through family albums with you, but the Bible passage and discussion may be too long for them. Instead, substitute Colossians 3:18-21, which makes the same points as the Ephesians passages but in a much shorter fashion.

ACTIVITY 2: Special Blend

Point: God made our family unique by placing each of us in it.

 Supplies: You'll need a different color of paint for each family member, toothpicks or paintbrushes to dip into the paint, white paper, and a Bible. If you don't have paint on hand, you can adapt this activity by using food coloring and milk.

Activity: Give each person a different color of paint and a toothpick or paintbrush. Begin with your own color. Let one drop of your color drip onto a sheet of white paper. Then have your spouse let one drop of his or her color drip into your drop. As your spouse does this, share one good quality your spouse brings to your family. For example, "Sharon brings enthusiasm to our family" or "Bill brings a listening ear to our family." If you like, let each family member share something positive they think this person adds to the family.

Use a toothpick or paintbrush to mix these colors together.

Then have each child add a drop of his or her color, mixing in this new addition. As with your spouse, share a good quality about each child, such as "Allison adds laughter to our family" or "Taylor brings a helpful attitude." Again, you may have other family members share their positive thoughts about this person, if you like.

When all family members have had a chance to add their color, ask these questions:

- **What new color was created?**
- **Can we ever go back to the original colors? Why or why not?**

Share: God made our family unlike any other. Even if another family has the same number of kids as ours or lives in a house like ours or even has our names, no other family is like ours. We're a special blend of people that God has put together! We've learned we each have special roles in our family, and that each person is special, but there's still more we can learn about living together as a family.

ACTIVITY 3: Stiff Support

Point: God made families to help each other.

 Supplies: You'll need masking tape, a bowl of unwrapped candies (such as M&M's or Skittles), a Bible, and either rulers, yardsticks, or sturdy towel rods. The sticks are needed to brace family member's elbows, keeping them straight. You might look around your house for other items that could be substituted as well, such as a length of pipe, a cardboard tube, or a similar sturdy item.

Have family members hold their arms out straight. On each person, place a ruler, yard-stick, or whatever sticklike item you've chosen on the inside of each elbow, then tape this in place. This should create a sturdy brace that prevents the arm from bending.

Note: It will be much less painful to remove the tape after the activity if family members wear long-sleeved shirts.

When each family member has been outfit-ted, have everyone sit around a table. Place a bowl of candy in the center of the table, and tell everyone they can eat as many as they like.

Because they're unable to bend their elbows, it will be difficult for family members to get food into their mouths. Kids may try rolling candies down their arms and eating them off their elbows. They may "cheat" and pick up a candy, set it on the table, then bend over and eat it off the table. Or you may observe other creative attempts.

Age Adjustments

OLDER CHILDREN AND TEENAGERS may be interested in going deeper on this topic and researching a bit about fam-ilies in the Bible. There are many examples of family relationships in the Old Testament, beginning with the very first family of Adam, Eve, Cain, and Abel. Study several of these families, then determine what made these families strong or weak. How did they treat each other? What was a result of their actions? How did the actions of the parents later affect the children? How was God able to use these families, or members of these families, even though they had prob-lems? What can we learn from Bible families?

See if family members discover they can easily feed each other, while they cannot feed themselves. If, after three or four minutes, they haven't figured this out, suggest they try feeding each other and see what happens then.

When everyone's eaten enough, put the candy aside and ask them these questions:

- **Besides eating, what are other activities you'd have trouble doing with your arms like this?** (Possible answers include writing, talking on the phone, driving, and cooking.)
- **If we all always wore these braces, what would we have to do for each other? How would we be able to survive?**
- **How is helping each other part of being a family?**
- **How can we help each other more day to day?**

Encourage your family to think of specific ways they already help each other or ways they can improve on helping each other. Your list might include helping each other with chores, with homework, or with other physical acts. You might also suggest helping each other with attitudes of encouragement, hugs, kind words, and other similar ideas.

 Read Proverbs 27:17 aloud and discuss:
  • **How does a knife become dull? How is it then sharpened?**

Share: A knife gets dull, or "unsharp," the more it's used. If you take one of our kitchen knives and carve wood with it, it's going to get dull and won't work very well the next time we want to cut meat with it. One way a knife can be sharpened is by rubbing it against another knife.
  • **How do we "sharpen" each other?** (Possible answers could be reading the Bible together, encouraging each other with kind words, keeping the attitude in our home positive, cheering for family members at their sporting events, defending family members when others are picking on them, and so on.)

Share: We can learn about God from the way we treat others in our family, and from the way they treat us. We can learn about how we should treat people outside our family as well. God made families so we could have a place to grow, practice what we're learning, and become strong and sharp!

WRAP-UP

Gather everyone in a circle and have family members take turns answering this question: **What's one thing you've learned about God today?**

Life Slogan: Today's Life Slogan is this: "God so loved me, He made my family!" Have family members repeat the slogan two or three times to help them learn it. Then encourage them to practice saying it during the week so they can talk about it at your next family night session.

Close in Prayer: Allow time for each family member to share prayer concerns and answers to prayer. Then close your time together with prayer for each concern. Thank God for making families, especially your family! Take time to thank God for each family member, mentioning one special quality you're thankful for about that person.

Remember to record your prayer requests so you can refer to them in the future as you see God answering them.

Additional Resources:

The Preschoolers Family Storybook by V. Gilbert Beers (ages 3–6)

ⓔ How to Lead
Your Child to Christ

SOME THINGS TO CONSIDER AHEAD OF TIME:

1. Realize that God is more concerned about your child's eternal destiny and happiness than you are. "The Lord is not slow in keeping his promise.... He is patient with you, not wanting anyone to perish, but everyone to come to repentance" (2 Peter 3:9).

2. Pray specifically beforehand that God will give you insights and wisdom in dealing with each child on his or her maturity level.

3. Don't use terms like "take Jesus into your heart," "dying and going to hell," and "accepting Christ as your personal Savior." Children are either too literal ("How does Jesus breathe in my heart?") or the words are too clichéd and trite for their understanding.

4. Deal with each child alone and don't be in a hurry. Make sure he or she understands. Discuss. Take your time.

A FEW CAUTIONS:

1. When drawing children to Himself, Jesus said for others to "allow" them to come to Him (see Mark 10:14). Only with adults did He use the term "compel" (see Luke 14:23). Do not compel children.

2. Remember that unless the Holy Spirit is speaking to the child, there will be no genuine heart experience of regeneration. Parents, don't get caught up in the idea that Jesus will return the day before you were going to speak to your child about salvation and that it will be too late. Look at God's character— He *is* love! He is not dangling your child's soul over hell. Wait on God's timing.

   Pray with faith, believing. Be concerned, but don't push.

THE PLAN:

1. **God loves you.** Recite John 3:16 with your child's name in place of "the world."

2. **Show the child his or her need of a Savior.**

   a. Deal with sin carefully. There is one thing that cannot enter heaven—sin.

   b. Be sure your child knows what sin is. Ask him to name some (things common to children—lying, sassing, disobeying, etc.). Sin is doing or thinking anything wrong according to God's Word. It is breaking God's Law.

   c. Ask the question "Have you sinned?" If the answer is no, do not continue. Urge him to come and talk to you again when he does feel that he has sinned. Dismiss him. You may want to have prayer first, however, thanking God "for this young child who is willing to do what is right." Make it easy for him to talk to you again, but do not continue. Do not say, "Oh, yes, you have too sinned!" and then name some. With children, wait for God's conviction.

   d. If the answer is yes, continue. He may even give a personal illustration of some sin he has done recently or one that has bothered him.

   e. Tell him what God says about sin: We've all sinned ("There is no one righteous, not even one," Rom. 3:10). And because of that sin, we can't get to God ("For the wages of sin is death . . . " Rom. 6:23). So He had to come to us (". . . but the gift of God is eternal life in Christ Jesus our Lord," Rom. 6:23).

   f. Relate God's gift of salvation to Christmas gifts—we don't earn them or pay for them; we just accept them and are thankful for them.

3. **Bring the child to a definite decision.**

   a. Christ must be received if salvation is to be possessed.

   b. Remember, do not force a decision.

   c. Ask the child to pray out loud in her own words. Give her some things she could say if she seems unsure. Now be prepared for a blessing! (It is best to avoid having the child repeat a memorized prayer after you. Let her think, and make it personal.)*

d. After salvation has occurred, pray for her out loud. This is a good way to pronounce a blessing on her.

4. **Lead your child into assurance.**

Show him that he will have to keep his relationship open with God through repentance and forgiveness (just like with his family or friends), but that God will always love him ("Never will I leave you; never will I forsake you," Heb. 13:5).

* If you wish to guide your child through the prayer, here is some suggested language.

> *"Dear God, I know that I am a sinner [have child name specific sins he or she acknowledged earlier, such as lying, stealing, disobeying, etc.]. I know that Jesus died on the cross to pay for all my sins. I ask you to forgive me of my sins. I believe that Jesus died for me and rose from the dead, and I accept Him as my Savior. Thank You for loving me. In Jesus' name. Amen."*

Cumulative Topical Index

TOPIC	SCRIPTURE	WHAT YOU'LL NEED	WHERE TO FIND IT
God Is Holy	Ex. 3:1-6	Masking tape, baby powder or corn starch, broom, Bible	Book 1, p. 31
God Is Invisible, Powerful and Real	John 1:18; 4:24; Luke 24:36-39	Balloons, balls, refrigerator magnets, Bible	Book 1, p. 15
God Knew His Plans for Us	Jer. 29:11	Two puzzles and a Bible	Book 2, p. 19
God Knows All About Us	Ps. 139:2-4; Matt. 10:30	3x5 cards, a pen	Book 2, p. 17
God Knows Everything	Isa. 40:13-14; Eph. 4:1-6	Bible	Book 1, p. 15
God Loves Us So Much, He Sent Jesus	John 3:16; Eph. 2:8-9	I.O.U. for each family member	Book 1, p. 34
God Made Our Family Unique by Placing Each of Us in It		Different color paint for each family member, toothpicks or paintbrushes to dip into paint, white paper, Bible	Book 2, p. 110
God Made Us in His Image	Gen. 1:24-27	Play dough or clay and Bible	Book 2, p. 24
God Provides a Way Out of Temptation	1 Cor. 10:12-13; James 1:13-14; 4:7; 1 John 2:15-17	Bible	Book 1, p. 88
God Wants Us to Get Closer to Him	James 4:8; 1 John 4:7-12	Hidden Bibles, clues to find them	Book 2, p. 33
God Will Send the Holy Spirit	John 14:23-26; 1 Cor. 2:12	Flashlights, small treats, Bible	Book 1, p. 39
God's Covenant with Noah	Gen. 8:13-21; 9:8-17	Bible, paper, crayons or markers	Book 2, p. 52
The Holy Spirit Helps Us	Eph. 1:17; John 14:15-17; Acts 1:1-11; 1:8; Eph. 3:16-17; Rom. 8:26-27; 1 Cor. 2:11-16; Eph. 1:17	Bible	Book 2, p. 99
Honor Your Parents	Ex. 20:12	Paper, pencil, treats, umbrella, soft objects, masking tape, pen, Bible	Book 1, p. 55
The Importance of Your Name Being Written in the Book of Life	Rev. 20:11-15; 21:27	Bible, phone book, access to other books with family name	Book 2, p. 74
It's Important to Listen to Jesus' Message		Bible	Book 2, p. 68

TOPIC	SCRIPTURE	WHAT YOU'LL NEED	WHERE TO FIND IT
Jesus Dies on the Cross	John 14:6	6-foot 2x4, 3-foot 2x4, hammers, nails, Bible	Book 1, p. 33
Jesus Took the Punishment We Deserve	Rom. 6:23; John 3:16; Rom. 5:8-9	Bathrobe, list of bad deeds	Book 1, p. 26
Jesus Washes His Followers' Feet	John 13:1-17	Bucket of warm, soapy water, towels, Bible	Book 1, p. 63
Joshua and the Battle of Jericho	Josh. 1:16-18; 6:1-21	Paper, pencil, dots on paper that when connected form a star	Book 1, p. 57
The More We Know God, the More We Know His Voice	John 10:1-6	Bible	Book 2, p. 35
Nicodemus Asks Jesus about Being Born Again	John 3:7, 50-51; 19:39-40	Bible, paper, pencil, costume	Book 2, p. 81
Obedience Has Good Rewards		Planned outing everyone will enjoy, directions on 3x5 cards, number cards	Book 1, p. 59
Parable of the Talents	Matt. 25:14-30	Bible	Book 1, p. 73
Parable of the Vine and Branches	John 15:1-8	Tree branch, paper, pencils, Bible	Book 1, p. 95
The Responsibilities of Families	Eph. 5:22-33; 6:1-4	Photo albums, Bible	Book 2, p. 101
Serve One Another in Love	Gal. 5:13	Bag of small candies, at least three per child	Book 1, p. 47
Sin Separates Humanity	Gen. 3:1-24	Bible, clay creations, piece of hardened clay or play dough	Book 2, p. 25
Some Places Aren't Open to Everyone		Book or magazine with "knock-knock" jokes	Book 2, p. 73
Some Things in Life Are Out of Our Control		Blindfolds	Book 2, p. 41
Temptation Takes Our Eyes Off God		Fishing pole, items to catch, timer, Bible	Book 1, p. 85
Those Who Don't Believe Are Foolish	Ps. 44:1	Ten small pieces of paper, pencil, Bible	Book 1, p. 19
The Tongue Is Small but Powerful	James 3:3-12	Video, news magazine or picture book showing devastation of fire, match, candle, Bible	Book 1, p. 77

TOPIC	SCRIPTURE	WHAT YOU'LL NEED	WHERE TO FIND IT
We All Sin	Rom. 3:23	Target and items to throw	Book 1, p. 23
We Can Communicate with Each Other			Book 2, p. 65
We Can Help Each Other	Prov. 27:17	Masking tape, bowl of unwrapped candies, rulers, yardsticks, or towel rods	Book 2, p. 110
We Can Love by Helping Those in Need	Heb. 13:1-3		Book 1, p. 48
We Can Show Love through Respecting Family Members		Paper and pen	Book 1, p. 66
We Can't Take Back the Damage of Our Words		Tube of toothpaste for each child, $10 bill	Book 1, p. 78
We Deserve Punishment for Our Sins	Rom. 6:23	Dessert, other materials as decided	Book 1, p. 24
We Have a New Life in Christ	John 3:3; 2 Cor. 5:17	Video or picture book of caterpillar forming a cocoon then a butterfly or a tadpole becoming a frog or a seed becoming a plant	Book 2, p. 93
We Know Others by Our Relationships with Them		Copies of questionnaire, pencils, Bible	Book 2, p. 31
We Must Choose to Obey		3x5 cards or slips of paper, markers and tape	Book 1, p. 43
We Must Learn How Much Responsibility We Can Handle		Building blocks, watch with second hand, paper, pencil	Book 1, p. 71
We Reap What We Sow	Gal. 6:7	Candy bar, Bible	Book 1, p. 55
With Help, Life Is a Lot Easier		Supplies to do the chore you choose	Book 2, p. 101
Wolves in Sheeps' Clothing	Matt. 7:15-20	Ten paper sacks, a marker, ten small items, Bible	Book 1, p. 97
You Look Like the Person in Whose Image You Are Created		Paper roll, crayons, markers, pictures of your kids and of yourself as a child	Book 2, p. 23

About
Heritage Builders

OUR VISION

To build a network of families, churches, and individuals committed to passing a strong family heritage to the next generation and to supporting one another in that effort.

OUR VALUES

Family—We believe that the traditional, intact family provides the most stable and healthy environment for passing a strong heritage to the next generation, but that non-intact homes can also successfully pass a solid heritage.

Faith—We believe that many of the principles for passing a solid heritage are effective regardless of one's religious tradition, but that the Christian faith provides the only lasting foundation upon which to build a strong family heritage.

Values—We believe that there are certain moral absolutes which govern our world and serve as the foundation upon which a strong heritage should be built, and that the current trend toward value neutrality is unraveling the heritage fabric of future generations.

Church—We believe that all families need a support network, and that the local church is the institution of choice for helping families successfully pass a strong heritage to the next generation.

OUR BELIEFS

We embrace the essential tenets of orthodox Christianity as summarized by the National Association of Evangelicals:

1. We believe the Bible to be the inspired, the only infallible, authoritative Word of God.

2. We believe that there is one God, eternally existent in three persons: Father, Son, and Holy Ghost.

3. *We believe in the deity of our Lord Jesus Christ, in His virgin birth, in His sinless life, in His miracles, in His vicarious and atoning death through His shed blood, in His bodily resurrection, in His ascension to the right hand of the Father, and in His personal return in power and glory.*

4. *We believe that for the salvation of lost and sinful people regeneration by the Holy Spirit is absolutely essential.*

5. *We believe in the present ministry of the Holy Spirit by whose indwelling the Christian is enabled to live a godly life.*

6. *We believe in the resurrection of both the saved and the lost; they that are saved unto the resurrection of life and they that are lost unot the resurrection of damnation.*

7. *We believe in the spiritual unity of believers in our Lord Jesus Christ.*

OUR PEOPLE

Heritage Builders is lead by a team of family life experts.

Cofounder - J. Otis Ledbetter, Ph.D.
Married over 25 years to Gail, two grown children, one teenager
Pastor, Chestnut Baptist Church in Clovis, California
Author - *The Heritage, Family Fragrance*

Cofounder - Kurt Bruner, M.A.
Married over 12 years to Olivia, two young sons
Vice President, Focus on the Family Resource Group
Author - *The Heritage, Family Night Tool Chest* Series

Cofounder - Jim Weidmann
Married over 15 years to Janet, two sons, two daughters
Family Night Training Consultant
Author - *Family Night Tool Chest* Series

Senior Associates - Heritage Builders draws upon the collective wisdom of various authors, teachers, and parents who provide resources, motivation, and advice for the heritage passing process.

BECOME A HERITAGE BUILDER IN YOUR COMMUNITY!

We seek to fulfill our mission by sponsoring the following.

HERITAGE BUILDERS RESOURCES - Products specifically designed to motivate and assist parents in the heritage passing process.

HERITAGE WORKSHOP - Using various formats, this seminar teaches attendees the principles and tools for passing a solid heritage, and helps them create a highly practical action plan for doing so.

HERITAGE BUILDERS NETWORK - A network of churches which have established an ongoing heritage builder support ministry where families can help families through mutual encouragement and creativity.

HERITAGE BUILDERS NEWSLETTER - We provide a forum through which families can share heritage building success stories and tips in our periodic newsletter.

If you are interested in hosting a Heritage Workshop, launching a Heritage Builders ministry in your local church, learning about new Heritage Building resources, receiving our newsletter, or becoming a Heritage Builder Associate, contact us by writing, phoning, or visiting our web site.

Heritage Builders
c/o ChariotVictor Publishing
4050 Lee Vance View
Colorado Springs, CO 80918
or call: 1-800-528-9489 (7 A.M.– 4:30 P.M. MST)
www.chariotvictor.com
or
www.heritagebuilders.com

HERITAGE BUILDERS

☐ Please send me a FREE One-Year Subscription to Heritage Builders Newsletter.

Name _____

Address _____

City _____ State _____ Zip _____ Phone _____

Church Affiliation _____

E-mail Address _____

Signature _____